Dedicated to:

Dr. Bahri and Lilly Gungor
and
Gerard and Elizabeth Griesbaum
Thank you for always loving, supporting, and believing in your kids.
You are deeply loved and appreciated!

THERE IS
MORE
TO THE
SECRET

THERE IS
MORE
TO THE
SECRET

Ed Gungor

THOMAS NELSON
Since 1798

NASHVILLE   DALLAS   MEXICO CITY   RIO DE JANEIRO   BEIJING

Published in Nashville, Tennessee, by Thomas Nelson, Inc.

Unless otherwise noted NIV, Scripture quotations are from the HOLY BIBLE: NEW INTERNATIONAL VERSION®. Copyright © 1973, 1978, 1984 by International Bible Society. Used by permission of Zondervan Publishing House. All rights reserved.

Scripture quotations noted AMP are from THE AMPLIFIED BIBLE: Old Testament. Copyright ©1962, 1964 by Zondervan Publishing House (used by permission).

Scripture quotations noted KJV are from The King James Version of the Bible.

Scripture quotations noted MSG are from *The Message* by Eugene H. Peterson, 1994, 1995, 1996, 2000. Copyright © 1993 Used by permission of NavPress Publishing Group. All rights reserved.

Scripture quotations noted NASB are from the NEW AMERICAN STANDARD BIBLE (R), © Copyright The Lockman Foundation 1960, 1962, 1963, 1968, 1971, 1972, 1973, 1975, 1977. Used by permission.

Scripture quotations noted NKJV are from THE NEW KING JAMES VERSION. Copyright © 1979, 1980, 1982, Thomas Nelson, Inc., Publishers.

Scripture quotations noted NLT are from the *Holy Bible*, New Living Translation, copyright © 1996. Used by permission of Tyndale House Publishers, Inc., Wheaton, Illinois 60189. All rights reserved.

Scripture quotations noted NLV are from The NEW LIFE Version. Copyright © 1969 © Christian Literature International.

The *International Children's Bible* (ICB)®, *New Century Version*®, copyright © 1986, 1988, 1999 by Thomas Nelson, Inc. Used by Permission.

The New Testament: A Translation in Modern English for Today's Reader by Olaf M. Norlie (NOR), © 1961 by Zondervan Publishing House.

Library of Congress Cataloging-in-Publication Data

Gungor, Ed.
  There is more to the secret : an examination of Rhonda Byrne's bestselling book "The secret".
    p. cm.
  ISBN-10: 0-8499-1978-9
  ISBN-13: 978-0-8499-1978-7
  1. Byrne, Rhonda. Secret. 2. Success. 3. Intentionalism. 4. Success—Religious aspects—Christianity.
I. W Publishing Group.
  BJ1611.2.T44 2007
  248.4—dc22   2007012354

Printed in the United States of America

07 08 09 10 11 RRD 5 4 3 2 1

Contents

Introduction

There Is More to "the Secret"

Of late, "the Secret" seems to be on everyone's lips. It is a belief that has been discovered and rediscovered all throughout history—and it is transforming. Understanding the law behind it changes everything. In her book *The Secret*, Rhonda Byrne and her team of contributors do a brilliant job of pulling together fragments of the great law that has been tucked away in oral traditions, in literature, and in religions and philosophies throughout the ages. They give us a life-transforming glance at this ancient truth.

But there is more to be told than this recent best-selling book has revealed. In fact, without a deeper look into the "more" I speak of, I fear that heartache may outweigh what help has been realized in people's lives.

That is the *why* of this writing. Though it is not my intention to tear down the good that has been communicated, we must proceed with caution. There is more to this story that must be told—*there is more to* "the Secret."

— Ed Gungor

1

Gods and Genies

OK. Before I get started, I have a confession to make. I'm an apprentice of Jesus Christ, and though I am a fan of Rhonda Byrne and her team's treatment of *the law of attraction*, I am a critical fan. I am very excited about what Byrne has communicated in the 2006 best-selling self-help book *The Secret*, and the film documentary of the same name. But at the same time, I do not start or end in the same philosophical place that the book does. For example, I do not believe that human beings are evolving into gods; we will always *need* God. Neither do I believe that humankind can self-save; we need a Savior. I believe that Jesus Christ knew this so-called secret, but he still had to die—the concept alone will not save us. Further, I feel that Byrne and company left too much room for material greed, social apathy, and the blaming of victims for the horrific events that occur in their lives. (I'm not suggesting that was their intention, but it is still a problem.) This does not mean, however, that I don't think the book has many good things to say—it does. In fact, I want to spend the bulk of this writing expanding on the treasure that it explores. We'll talk about the problems as we go along.

What Is It?

We only have one shot at life. Consequently, I think we should write our lives *large*—we should decide to matter. This idea helps us do that. It touches every aspect of our lives—from our finances to our health to our relationships. When understood, it unearths the hidden, untapped power within each of us—pagan or saint.

This is not some complex, hard-to-grasp idea. It is simply the law of attraction. This law, plainly stated, is: *Everything coming into your life is the result of what you have been attracting to your life.* Your life is not the way it is by accident; it is the product of cause and effect. In a sense, how you live your life is a magnet, which draws the events that occur *into* your life—both good and bad.

Though this may sound scary at first (*everything is my fault?*), what a great discovery it is! This means that you and I have a lot to say about how happy our lives can be. When we learn how the law of attraction works, we can "work it" to keep the good things we enjoy coming into our lives while refusing access to the bad things.

But is that really possible?

There are many who believe that whatever is *destined* to be, *will be.* They think that humans have nothing to do with the future; that is *God's* sphere. Things only happen, these folks contend, because of God's sovereignty, and human beings don't really cause anything to happen that God wouldn't have done anyway. This group would argue that our thoughts, beliefs, and actions are more of an aside, because God will do what God will do, irrespective of what humans do.

But if God had really wanted to create a world where humans *couldn't* control things, then why did he create a world filled with laws—laws so specific and predictable that we can send a person to the moon and predict within a fraction of a second when he or she will land there? What if God created laws precisely so that we humans could have *more* control over our lives? The great apostle Paul claimed, "All things are yours, whether . . . the world or life or death or the present or the future—all are yours."[1] In another place he wrote, "Do not be deceived: God cannot be mocked. A man reaps what he sows."[2]

These texts assert that the way we participate in the world God created is much the same way a farmer participates with the laws of nature. A farmer who wants the earth to yield a corn crop must learn to cooperate with nature to get it. Nature does not select the kind of harvest—it waits for the farmer to decide. The farmer makes that choice. He predicts the field's future by the kind of seed that is sown there. To "attract" corn, the farmer simply plants corn seed. This is the way the law of attraction works.

Creation works the same way for you and me. God doesn't determine on his own how wonderful our lives are. To some degree, *we* control the level of success that we enjoy in our marriages, finances, careers, parenting, etc., based on whether or not we cooperate with the laws God placed here. We can have happiness or heartache, *on purpose.* We can attract whatever it is that we want to attract—the truth is, we are doing that *now.* Learning how this law works doesn't make it work—it works all the time—but learning how it works helps us to "work it" to our advantage instead of to our disadvantage.

Newton's third law of motion states: *For every action, there is an equal and opposite reaction.* This is another way to express the law of attraction. Jesus Christ showed us how the law of attraction, aka "the Secret," works in our relationships with others: "Do not judge, and you will not be judged; and do not condemn, and you will not be condemned; pardon, and you will be pardoned. Give, and it will be given to you. They will pour into your lap a good measure—pressed down, shaken together, and running over. For by your standard of measure it will be measured to you in return."[3]

This means that if you smile at someone, he most likely will smile right back. If you are mean to a person, chances are, she will be mean to you. If you are genuine and kind to others, you are almost certain to have others express kindness in return. If you are critical of everything and everyone, you can expect a hefty dose of critical judgment from others in your life. You *attract* what you put out. The law of attraction is at work for everyone, everywhere, all the time, whether one understands it or not.

Believers in God often get mixed up on the balance between the things *we* are to do and the things God does. There is a story of a rancher out west who received a visit from his pastor. As the rancher showed the preacher around the property, with its well-maintained outbuildings, fences, and manicured lawns, the pastor declared rather piously, "My, how God has blessed this property!"

In a straightforward manner the rancher replied, "I guess . . . but you should have seen it when he had it all by himself."

If we are not careful, those of us who are God-followers will be guilty of something Jesus Christ warned us about. In his parable of the talents (Matt. 25:14–29), he urged people to work with the potential they had been given by God. But he said that some would be so oriented to the sovereignty of God that they would basically do nothing and resign themselves to fate. In other words, they'd join the Doris Day crowd, singing, "Que será será, whatever will be, will be . . ." Jesus said that this bunch believed that God, like the master in his story, harvests what he has "not sown" and gathers where he has "not scattered seed." In other words, humans don't have to do *jack*—God does it all. Jesus said this group buried their potential "in the ground" (v. 25)—and God was not happy about it.

But there is danger on both sides of this issue.

Proponents of the latest usage of the law of attraction claim that it gives us everything we could ever desire—happiness, health, and wealth; that we can do or be anything we want; and that we can possess anything we choose—no matter how big. We are asked, "What kind of home do you want to live in?" or, "Do you want to be a millionaire?" We are told, "Miracles happen when you know how to apply the '*Secret*.'" American poet Ralph Waldo Emerson (1803–1882) once wrote, "The secret is the answer to all that has been, all that is, and all that will ever be." Quoting Emerson, advocates of the beliefs I just described claim that the great secret of life is this: each of us works with one infinite power—the law of attraction.

But they leave out a very critical piece. It turns out that *there is more to the "Secret."*

We Share the Power

When personal computers first appeared in the 1980s, installing new programs or peripherals (like printers or scanners) was more than a "plug-and-play" event. It wasn't unusual for your whole computer to stop working after adding a new program that was *supposed* to make life easier. Then you would have to spend hours on the phone with the software provider's "help desk" as a technician walked you through the arduous process of rewriting hidden program lines (such as CON-FIG.SYS). It was a mess.

The reason there were so many problems is that software developers designed their software on PCs that contained *no other programs.* Hence, they could marshal all their PCs' resources for the execution of the programs *they* were developing. Not a bad thing to do—if all PCs ran only *one* program. But they don't. But that didn't stop the engineers from altering their computers' internal codes in order to most efficiently run their own programs. It was a dog-eat-dog, every-company-for-itself programming world. And as consumers began to load one new program after another onto their computers, applications began to conflict with one another, fighting for limited internal resources, and systems began to lock up. (I wish I had a dollar for every hour I have spent on the phone line with "Technical Support," clearing up "conflicts.") We've come a long way, baby.

As Byrne and her associates lay out the anatomy of *The Secret,* I can't help but feel that they are making a mistake similar to that of the early PC program developers. The repeated emphasis in their treatment of the idea is on each person's *individual* power and control while using the law of attraction. The problem is, there isn't just *one* person using that law—more than *one* program is running in the universe. We don't use the law of attraction in a vacuum—there are other players, other forces in motion.

For example, in the book the Byrne team claims that we attract *everything* that happens to us—even the bad things, like car accidents. While that may be true in some cases, it is an oversimplification of reality.

Consider the Holocaust. Is it really plausible that six million Jews all "attracted" this unimaginable horror into their lives, all on their own? Or were there other forces in play—such as unlimited power in the hands of an insane dictator named Hitler? And what about the abuse and murder of children? Did the victims "imagine" and "attract" those things to themselves? If not, then why did it happen to them? Did the law of attraction that "works for all people everywhere at all times" *not* work in their case, or are there other forces in motion—like a sick perpetrator?

And what about God? Supporters of today's practice of the law of attraction are almost silent about him. That's odd when you consider that most people believe in God. In their iteration of The Secret, Byrne's group seems to hold to the notion that *if* God created what is, then he is certainly no longer present in it—at least not in any relevant way. There is no "Big Plan." And if God does exist, then he (or she?) is apparently distant and unknowable—living well outside the affairs of the world, which do not or cannot touch him. They suggest that the universe is instead a kind of *genie* that exists purely to grant our every wish—our wish is Genie's command. And "Genie" is granting wishes *at this very moment*—good ones and bad ones. Understanding this idea, they say, is the key to getting the universe to grant you only the good wishes.

This Is God's Story

In the Christian tradition, there are no genies. Each person is a dream of God come true; a destiny; a planned and purposeful being that God placed in the world as a unique character in his unfolding story. Scripture claims that God "determined the times" in which we would be born and planned "the exact places" that we would live.[4] The psalmist declared, "All the days ordained for me were written in your book before one of them came to be."[5]

This means that each one of us matters, and how we fit in this world works toward a *telos*—an "end"—of a goal-directed process concocted by God himself. For God-followers, this isn't a land for the "survival of the fittest"—it is a world for the predestined. But instead of looking for God's predestined plan, many think they are making up their own story. Contrary to what Byrne tells us, the *secret* tucked away in history involved human beings, not making up their own stories but finding their places in the story being told by someone else—God. The most ancient revealing of this fact viewed creation as *full* of God's purposeful ideas—there was a place for *everything* and *everyone*. The law of attraction wasn't used to attract just anything; it was used to attract the telos of God. It revealed that each of us is born into God's world and that it is *his* stage; we are but participants in *his play*. The psalmist said, "Know that the LORD is God. It is he who made us, and we are his."[6]

My wife, Gail, and I recently went to a play featuring our beautiful daughter-in-law, Erin. She had one of the lead roles. After the show, we showered her with kudos and asked her how she felt the performance went. In response, she talked mainly about how she thought *she* did with *her* role. There was no complaining about the others onstage, no wishing that she'd had their lines, no attempt on her part to take over another's role, and no discussion of how she wished she could rewrite the script or direct the show differently. She measured her success by how well she performed the job *assigned* to her.

This is how we should hit the stage of life. This is central to the idea—and the very reason why God created the law of attraction. We should refuse to try to write, produce, direct, or choose the part we want to perform in our own play. We need to see God as the Writer, Producer, and Director. Our ambition should be to discover our individual, God-destined role and then perform that role large.

Somehow realizing that we are here to cooperate in something bigger than ourselves gives us a bridge to a transcendent life—access to an existence that is bigger than one of our own crafting, larger than the immediate desires of selfish people, with their ever-expanding needs. This "roots" us in something grander, something bigger, something eternal.

In a dog-eat-dog, every-man-for-himself world, where nothing is more important than *number one*, searching for God's telos is seen as irrelevant, because it is connected to something other than *self*. But this discovery gives a new self-worth based on an identity valued by God—it links our personal competency to fruitfulness for more than just ourselves. This doesn't deplete us as persons; it leads us to God. And our sense of identity is emboldened through union with Life larger than oneself.

This is how we participate in what is referred to as the kingdom of God. We anticipate that God will act; we expect God to act. We just don't know where or when. But we listen, and we continue to walk in the law of attraction as a gesture of our love and pursuit of God. A life committed to discovering a telos created by God gradually fills us with a spirit of expectation that all good things will be given to the obedient heart—we will eat "the fat of the land."[7] Jesus says that it is when we are willing to lose our lives (in God's telos) that we find them.[8]

A commitment to God's telos gives us a deep sense of personal meaning and vocation. We become cheerful participants in the scheme of creation and of God's providence that grounds us in a sense of purpose and dedication. It is our rabid individualization that has left us, as British historian Arnold Toynbee so aptly put it, with a "sense of having all we need and still feeling alienated."[9]

The currency at stake here is, who is the initiator in life—God or man? Many modern Christians have adapted the popular motivational speakers' views of the human person: We dream and then do whatever we want to. And we expect God to bless it, to make it great. Yes, there the law of attraction works, and we can expect greatness when we sow for greatness. But the Bible also gives us warnings about this. We are told not to run impulsively with our own plans, because our life is "a mist that appears for a little while and then vanishes."[10] We are here for too short a time to cultivate enough wisdom to make life decisions on our own. "Instead," the text explains, "you ought to say, If it is the Lord's will, we will live and do this or that."[11] That means that you and I can play a significant role—we can enjoy great success—but we don't get to write our own play. We are in God's story; he should initiate or at least carry the right of veto on life's plans.

Many church people carry their own agendas and cultivate self-actualizing dreams, believing that if they just add a dab of faith to their dreaming, they may receive from God the extra "luck" they need to get the fame, power, and wealth that they want. It is true that the Scriptures teach, "Everything is possible for him who believes,"[12] but if we are not careful, we end up a stone's throw away from reducing God to our servant. Our own desires quickly become the center of the universe.

Thinking of God as a genie is dangerous. We need to let God be God and realize genies only exist in fairytales.

2

Thoughts Become Things

In Rhonda Byrne's book *The Secret*, she asserts that everything coming into your life is being attracted to your life via the law of attraction. Further, things are attracted to you by the images that you hold in your mind. That would mean what you think about and ponder really does *matter*. If this is true, then you should take special note of your thoughts, because whatever is going through your mind is being attracted to you.

But is there any evidence of this in Scripture?

The answer is a resounding "YES!" The ancient Hebrew proverb asserts, "As a man thinks in his heart, so is he."[1] This means you will become what you think about the most. It is as if our thoughts are a magnet, drawing the very things we are thinking of *into* our lives. In other words, "if you see it in your mind, you are going to hold it in your hand."[2] And the clearer your mind is about the things you want, the speedier they will move toward you.

This idea is summed up in three simple words: *Thoughts become things.*[3] They hold an intrinsic creative power. The first creative event ever recorded was in Genesis 1; God created the universe with a command—with his *words*. Words are simply thoughts expressed. The universe is here because God thought of it. We are here because God thought of us. Because we are the only creatures in the world created in God's likeness, we, too, can creatively *think*, that is, we can participate in creative events—we can enjoy the fruit of the law of attraction.

Artists, architects, musicians, craftspersons, entrepreneurs, friends, lovers, everyday Joes and Janes, butchers, bakers, and candlestick makers—all of us get to be creative because we can think. Sure, we may not be able to create solar systems or make things out of nothing, but the creative capacity was placed in our souls by the Creator himself. And the whole process happens in the domain of *thoughts.*

This is why there is so much spiritual warfare surrounding a person's thought life. God invites us to take on his thoughts, while Scripture claims that an "enemy" of our souls is trying to influence us with his evil imaginations. It declares, "Satan, who is the god of this world, has blinded the minds of those who don't believe."[4] Satan influences thought. Why? If he can influence our thoughts, then he can affect what we attract into our lives. It turns out that Satan and the forces of darkness are responsible for much of the heartache and trouble people find in their lives and relationships.[5]

God, on the other hand, calls us to take on *his* thoughts. "My thoughts are not your thoughts," he says in Isaiah 55:8, and he invites us to think as he thinks. This is why we are to give the Bible a place in our lives—it is God's Word, his thoughts. We are invited to take in God's thoughts so that we can step above our own limited thinking and begin to attract life of a higher order—*eternal life*. We are not just afforded peace; we are offered the peace of God. We are not just furnished joy; we can partake in the joy of the Lord. The apostle Peter claimed that by embracing the thoughts of God, we actually "participate in the divine nature."[6] How sweet is that?

When you consider Satan's attempts to "blind" our thoughts versus God's call for us to adopt his thoughts, you have the makings of a knock-down, drag-out fight. But, Paul states, "We use the things God gives to fight with and they have power. Those things God gives to fight with destroy the strong-places of the devil. We break down *every thought* . . . that puts itself up against the wisdom of God. We take hold of *every thought* and make it obey Christ."[7]

We are to fight over which thoughts are and are not welcome in our minds, because our thoughts *matter*. Our minds are not just passive holding zones, forced to think about whatever pops into them. We get to choose the thoughts we have, and we should fight hard, using the "things God gives to fight with" for this right. Paul wrote, "You'll do best by filling your minds and meditating on things true, noble, reputable, authentic, compelling, gracious—the best, not the worst; the beautiful, not the ugly; things to praise, not things to curse."[8]

Byrne and her contributors claim that thoughts have a "frequency" associated with them, and when you think of a particular thing, it emits a frequency that draws that thing back to you. These thought frequencies draw what you are thinking of back to you. If you think *abundance*, abundance will come to you. If you think *lack*, lack will find its way back to you. And this works for every person, all the time.

I don't know if that is the anatomy of how it works, but there is certainly something at work when you think—this law of attraction functions through what is going on in our minds, and the law is obedient to our thoughts. If you are focusing on things you want, the law of attraction kicks in and gives you what you desire. Contrariwise, if you focus on what you don't want, the law of attraction will call that into existence as well. The law doesn't hear that you don't want it. It is simply obeying you, manifesting what you are imagining. And it always does so.

This may help: the law of attraction is simply a reiteration of the law of sowing and reaping. You reap what you sow. The law isn't biased—it doesn't judge whether or not you are worthy of what you reap. It just works with what you sow. Put wheat seed into the ground and you will get wheat seed back. Similarly, when you sow seeds of fear into your mind and you will reap fear-filled events. In the midst of the horrible events that the biblical character Job went through, he declared, "What I feared has come upon me; what I dreaded has happened to me."[9]

However this works, it is *always* working. It works as you think. Thoughts are always creating reality, and when you have a chronic way of thinking, you are in the *creation process*. Something is going to manifest out of those thoughts—whether good or bad.

This suggests that many of the problems that occur in people's lives come because they tend to dwell only on the things they *don't* want. That is why those things keep coming back to them over and over again. Their chronic negative thinking pulls chronic negative things into their lives. When you focus on the negative, it comes to you again and again. To have new experiences, you have to think different thoughts. You have to change your focus. Albert Einstein said, "The significant problems we face cannot be solved at the same level of thinking we were at when we created them." Well said, Albert.

Most of us need a new level of thinking. We are used to looking on the negative side of things and have habitually practiced an expectation of dread. When addressing the need to develop new thinking patterns, Byrne's team suggests that people simply focus on things they want, from parking spaces to healthy, loving relationships. They also urge folks to recall pleasant memories or get out into nature or listen to their favorite music. And from these simple suggestions, testimonies are pouring in from all over the world of transformed lives.

Byrne writes:

As the film swept the world, stories of miracles began to flood in: people wrote about healing from chronic pain, depression, and disease; walking for the first time after an accident, even recovering from a deathbed. We have received thousands of accounts of *The Secret* being used to bring about large sums of money and unexpected checks in the mail. People have used *The Secret* to manifest their perfect homes, life partners, cars, jobs, and promotions, with many accounts of businesses being transformed within days of applying *The Secret.* There have been heartwarming stories of stressed relationships involving children being restored to harmony.[10]

Believe it or not, this has made some believers in Christ angry. How can people have changed lives without Christ being preached? they want to know. It *is* possible for those who believe right things to have wrong emotions (anger, jealousy, pride). We get angry because we tend to divide the world into the haves and have-nots; those who are good and those who are evil, those in the right and those in the wrong—and we do it with very clear boundaries, piercing stares, and long, pointy fingers. Because the direct preaching of Christ is not present in Byrne's presentation, we assume that proponents of her ideas (and perhaps the ideas themselves) must be evil—belonging to the have-nots' crowd.

But what if that is an oversimplification and simply not true?

Here is a chunk of profound Christian theology: everything that God created is good.[11] That means that there is a basic holiness present in every*thing* and every*one.* That is not to say that there is not corruption. When I was a kid in Wisconsin, we had an old, rusty car that was "see-throughish" in spots. It was corrupted. It wasn't pretty. But it *did* work. There was *some* good to it. Things and people in a fallen world are like old cars—we have some good, but we're also *see-throughish*.

N. T. Wright says it best:

The line between good and evil is never simply between "us" and "them." The line between good and evil runs through each one of us. There is such a thing as wickedness, and we must distinguish between small and low-grade versions of it and large and terrible versions of it. We must not make the trivial mistake of supposing that a one-off petty thief and a Hitler are exactly alike, that the same level of evil is attained by someone who cheats in an exam and by a Bin Ladin. But nor must we suppose that the problem of evil can be either addressed or solved if we trivialize it in the other way, of labeling some people "good" and other people "bad."[12]

Those of us who are God-followers run toward him precisely because he is *good*, and we want goodness to be the prevailing force in our lives. But the point is, just because the self-help gurus don't contextualize the law of attraction inside the gospel of Christ does not mean they are evil people and part of the wrong, "have-not" crowd. It *does* mean that they are missing a huge part of the story. It also means that they are being reckless and, in my opinion, even enabling (at some points) to forms of evil (more on that later). But they are not necessarily wicked people who should be discounted out of hand. They actually offer some profound principles to consider—principles that Christians would do well to heed.

Common Grace

So, why does this ancient practice work for everyone—even those without faith in God? Because the law of attraction is a law of *common grace*. Let me explain.

God loves the world he created. He sees the value and preciousness of all things and all people. He made the world because he wanted to be a part of it—to flood his own life into it. We know by reading the end of the Bible that God will eventually move into his creation.[13] God is a part of it all both *generally* (common grace) and *redemptively* (salvation grace).

Common grace is that grace or "favor" (*grace* literally means "unmerited favor") that is poured out on all people everywhere. Common grace provides all the good that we know: land, seasons, rain, sunshine, harvest, beauty, love, family, friendship, etc. Jesus said, "This is what God does. He gives his best—the sun to warm and the rain to nourish—to everyone, regardless: the good and bad, the nice and nasty."[14] Once, while the apostle Paul was preaching to pagans who had never heard of Jesus, he exclaimed, "In the generations before us, God let all the different nations go their own way. But even then he didn't leave them without a clue, for he made a good creation, poured down rain and gave bumper crops. When your bellies were full and your hearts happy, there was evidence of good beyond your doing."[15]

God does "good beyond your doing." This is common grace. In front of another non-Christian group, Paul proclaimed, "[God] himself gives life and breath to everything, and he satisfies every need."[16] Common grace is God's engaging in the world, making it better for all humankind, irrespective of whether or not they believe in him. Medicine and technology are, I think, samplers of common grace.

I live in Oklahoma. We are part of what's known as "tornado alley." During our monstrous storms, I turn on the TV and watch how storm trackers can pinpoint a twister's exact location with something they call Doppler radar. I always think, *Thank you, God. Thank you for making this world safer and sweeter by giving people wisdom of how the laws of nature work!* This is common grace, God's love in motion for "the good and bad, the nice and nasty."

The law of attraction is smack in the middle of the domain of common grace. God is still involved—but you don't have to recognize that God is involved to experience the benefit of common grace. He is involved when you plant a garden, fall in love, giggle at a joke, or sense fulfillment upon completing a project. He is in all the good we experience. And he is involved as you experience the physical manifestations of what goes on in your head through the law of attraction.

The good news is—*there is more.* God also has *redemptive grace.* This is where we encounter God on a much more direct level. We experience his presence, his forgiveness, and the fruit of the Holy Spirit; we gain access to his promises; and we share in his eternal life. Certainly, this beats any job promotion or new car or anything else the common law of attraction can bring to you. However, they are tied together. The quickest road to discovering redemptive grace is by acknowledging that God is the source of common grace. In other words, praise God for all the good in your life.

The reason it is critical for humans to "praise God" is not because God is on some kind of ego trip. Praising God is simply recognizing that he is responsible for all the good we know. I have been praised for jobs I have done. It is a form of thanks. When we do this to God—when we acknowledge him for common grace—it opens the door for us to taste redemptive grace—which is common grace on steroids! (We'll come back to this later.)

We Are Michelangelos

When you realize God designed your quality of life to be directly connected to your predominate thoughts, you will become more careful about what you think. It's amazing to discover that you are the one drawing into your life the people, the jobs, your circumstances, your health, your wealth, the debt, the joy—everything. This law mandates that what we entertain in our minds comes to us—we draw it to ourselves as a magnet pulls on metal. In other words, *whatever we think about, we bring about.*

Thoughts become like the chisel in our hands. When Michelangelo carved the *David* statue, he was the one in charge of the image that was to appear. Similarly, the quality of our emotions, our relationships, our careers—basically everything we touch—can be intentionally carved by understanding and cooperating with the law of attraction; we can be our own Michelangelos. God is not the one holding you back or trying to dampen your life. He gave us life as a gift. He wants us to learn how to master it, as we do any of the other laws of nature, to our benefit.

Imagine learning to live well; learning to get better at being happy, as farmers have gotten better at growing crops; learning how to discuss differences in our relationships, as doctors have learned how to perform surgeries less invasively and with quicker recovery times. This is the great secret, and we have got to learn how to cooperate with it. We must start expecting good things to happen instead of dreading the worst. We need to be more hopeful and less worrywartish. And this is available to everyone—even those without faith!

Add redemptive grace, through your faith in Christ, on top of your knowledge of the law of attraction, and get ready for real life, the kind that Jesus describes, wherein, "everything is possible for him who believes,"[17] and "whatever you ask for in prayer, believe that you have received it, and it will be yours."[18]

What kind of lives would we live if we mastered common grace and used our faith to run after redemptive grace? We would probably look like sons and daughters of God. We'd be jammed with hope, filled with affection for others, exuberant about life, calm, flooded with compassion, steady with the difficult, convinced of God's good in every person and every thing (though aware of the corruption), involved with loyal commitments, shy about forcing our way in life, and able to marshal and direct our energies wisely. To be sure, life would be sweet. And ever so much sweeter than what proponents of today's usage of the law of attraction suggest. Let *them* fixate on that narrow range of middle-class concerns: houses, cars, and expensive vacations—with loved ones and the rest of humanity somewhere in the back of the pack (only attended to if they make *them* feel good). These folks just *think* they're using the law of attraction. Believers *really* get to use it. Let's take a closer look at how, next.

3

Using the Law of Attraction

Why do things happen the way they do in our lives? Why do people treat us the way they do? Why do some folks seem to experience consistent good fortune, while others appear cursed? Is it fate? Or are there other forces at work in the world? Do good things happen to some and bad things to others because God loves some but is ticked off at others?

Though I am not willing to buy into the idea that we control *everything* by utilizing the law of attraction, I do believe that we are in control of a whole lot more than most people think. And the Secret affords us the knowledge to take more control.

Winston Churchill said, "You create your own universe as you go along." What if that is true? What if human beings, who are in God's image, are designed by God to be part of the creative process?

In her book *The Secret*, Rhonda Byrne claims that we have the power to change *anything*, and we do so by choosing the thoughts we think and by feeling the feelings that we feel. She maintains that we draw the things that come into our lives by our prolonged thoughts and persistent feelings.

What if there is really something to this?

I can think of so many times that this has played out in my life. Every time I prepare for a new series of messages in the church I pastor, I notice that I run into conversations, articles, or TV shows that deal with exactly what I am preparing to speak on. How many times have you heard a sermon and were struck by the fact that you had *just* been thinking about that issue? It seemed, in fact, as if the pastor was reading your mind?

How many times has someone crossed your mind that you hadn't thought of in a while? Then, within just a few days, someone talks to you about that very person, or you actually hear from him or her?

What is going on? Is it all just happenstance, or is there some kind of aura that floats out into the world, drawing people and things that you think of back to you? Imagining that thoughts work in this way certainly gives the process vividness and tangibility. It makes it more *real.* The possibility that your thoughts and feelings are actually being transmitted into the world and drawing back the very things you were thinking and feeling is a pretty wild concept.

How It Works

I have to admit it sounds fantastical to me when Byrne and her team speak with scientific certainty about how this all works, when they are really just *guessing.* The scientific foundations of their claims are clearly dubious—how can one prove the notion that thoughts emit a frequency that draws the physical counterpart of that thought back to you. But Byrne writes, "You are like a human transmission tower, transmitting a frequency with your thoughts."[1]

I don't think the book is really trying to prove its hypothesis of how the law of attraction works as much as it is trying to make the concept more tangible and accessible for people. And, though you may feel awkward about the "transmission" schema, you shouldn't be offended and reject what is being said because of it.

Christ-followers are often afraid of attempting to understand what we consider to be matters of faith. The truth is, we are content to leave much of what we believe in the domain of "mystery." We think that matters of faith should remain *unknowable*. Trying to explain processes that are currently unknowable violates our sensibility of *mystery* and *faith*, so we tend to label any attempt to do so as "crazy," or "of the devil," or a "New Age heresy." But just because we haven't considered concrete ways that things happen in our lives doesn't mean that to try is crazy or of the devil or a New Age heresy. *Take a chill pill.* I think it would do us good to try to hypothesize about possible ways that such things actually function.

Consider prayer. How in the world does it work? We just believe it does. But what if we talked about *how* it worked—the physical nature of it? Could there be some kind of energy that radiates from our souls to God—something that is tangible and perceptible to him? Scripture claims that in heaven there are "golden bowls full of incense, which are the prayers of the saints."[2] What if that is literal?

What if our prayers can, in fact, be captured by God and placed in actual "bowls"? Imagine that the next time you pray.

Paul calls the believer "the aroma of Christ" and "the fragrance of life."[3] What if that is *literally true* in the realm of the eternal? (That would mean that God smells us, and we smell good.) Just because we can't see how these things work doesn't mean that there isn't an actual way that it does. And though we have no way to measure these things now, what if, in the future, we are able?

God created the whole universe, using laws that have taken us millennia to figure out. We have just recently begun to understand weather patterns, deep space, the human genome, and the wonders of the human body. The 1990s were called the "decade of the brain," as scientists discovered wagonloads of new facts about how our brains work. We now know that feelings of stress or joy or dread or fear are actually associated with measurable chemical and electrical processes in our brains! What if in the future we will be able to detect some kind of "energy field" that demonstrates the physical functionality of the law of attraction? Religious folks need to quit being so high-strung and nervous about new discoveries and ideas.

If anyone should be open, it should be believers. After all, we can feel safe as we explore things, because we are tethered to Scripture.

Biblical Evidence

Believe it or not, there is Scriptural evidence for some kind of physical activity taking place as we think, feel, and act in the world. In the book of Jeremiah, the Hebrew word *ra'a* is used ninety times. For Jeremiah, ra'a was the entity that God was taking special note of as it emerged from his people, Israel. Theologian Klaus Koch explains: "[Ra'a] is an aura, with effects on the world, an aura encircling the particular agent, who brings about his own destiny."[4] Jeremiah saw the ra'a as a sort of transmission of the emotional and spiritual condition of Israel that went out into the world and then returned to Israel with the fruit of that condition.

This is why Jeremiah declared to the people, "It's the way you've lived that's brought all this on you. The bitter taste is from your evil life. That's what's piercing your heart."[5] The ra'a was drawing horribly negative things back into their lives.

Is it really so hard to imagine that many of the circumstances in your life are literally being affected by forces that lie within *you*? And if that is true, shouldn't you make it a priority to learn how to marshal those forces?

Managing Your Thoughts

If your thoughts are pulling things toward you, then you obviously want to stop thinking bad thoughts. Fearful, dread-filled, sinful, hateful, mean, lack-oriented, shame-based *thoughts* bring fearful, dreadful, sinful, hateful, mean, lack-filled, shameful *experiences* back to you. The old Sunday school song goes, "Oh, be careful little mind what you think . . ." No kidding.

So how in the world do you start to get a handle on your thought life? Researchers tell us that we have tens of thousands of thoughts a day. Trying to control all those thoughts would be impossible. But here's some good news, your emotions are indicators of your thoughts. If you feel good, you are thinking good thoughts. If you feel bad, you are thinking bad thoughts. Feelings are like newspaper headlines— they tell you what the story is about; they "headline" the fine print of your thought life.

Though this statement is an oversimplification, a shortcut to using the law of attraction to your advantage is to *do* the things that you feel good about, and *avoid* doing what you don't feel good about. (If you are a Christ-follower and you are thinking ahead, you already see the problems with this view—but hang in there. We'll get to that in a bit.)

Byrne and contributors repeatedly hammer this point home:

You have two sets of feelings: good feelings and bad feelings. And you know the difference between the two because one makes you feel good, and the other makes you feel bad. It's the depression, it's the anger, it's the resentment, it's the guilt. It's those feelings that don't make you feel empowered. The flipside is that you have good emotions and good feelings. You know when they come because they make you feel good. Excitement, joy, gratitude, love. Imagine if we could feel that way every day. When you celebrate the good feeling, you'll draw to you more good feelings, and things that make you feel good.[6]

Byrne asserts that your thoughts produce a "frequency," and your feelings tell you immediately what frequency you are on. When you are feeling bad, you are on the frequency that draws more bad to you. The law of attraction works to ensure you experience more of what you are currently feeling—good or bad.

The bottom line is, we must learn to pay attention to our feelings. Learning to manage feelings is much easier than trying to manage thousands of thoughts. However, *there is more to this Secret.*

The Hard Places

I get that the Byrne team wants to encourage us to attract good things: "If you're feeling good, then you're creating a future that's on track with your desires. If you're feeling bad, you're creating a future that's off track with your desires."[7] But then they make radical statements like, "When I really understood that my primary aim was to feel and experience joy, then I began to do *only those things which brought me joy.* I have a saying: 'If it ain't fun, don't do it!'"[8]

How exactly does *that* work? How do you only do things that are fun? Byrnes repeatedly urges us to only do the things that we love to do, while avoiding the things that we *don't* love to do. At one point we are even told, "If you experience joy eating a salami sandwich, then do that!"[9]

OK. So what if I really like eating salami sandwiches—so much so that I clog my arteries and have a heart attack? Is that really *fun?*

It seems to me that in an attempt to make this simple, fans of today's usage of the law of attraction are opening a kind of Pandora's box. There are two kinds of fun, two kinds of joy. There is the fun of eating what you want and being a couch potato, and there is the fun of the good health that comes after you participate in the pain of working out and eating right. There is the fun of going out each night with friends, attending movies, playing cards, and yukking it up, and then there is the fun of getting a great job because you suffered through the anguish of getting an education, reading boring books, and agonizing over those term papers.

Just because something is difficult and uncomfortable in the short term doesn't mean you should avoid it. Often short-term pain yields long-term gain. If your "take away" from the law of attraction is *do whatever feels good now,* then you are headed for a life of heartache. Decades ago, W. Beran Wolfe wrote:

If you have evaded all unpleasantness in your life your happiness is placed in unstable equilibrium by the constant dread that some unavoidable disappointment is just around the corner. If you have faced pain and disappointment, you not only value your happiness more highly, but you are prepared for [the] unpredictable. There may be many happy human vegetables who have succeeded in avoiding unhappiness and pain, but they cannot call themselves human.[10]

So much of the good stuff can only be had *after* you have walked through the "land of hard." Instead of avoiding something that makes you feel bad, ponder on whether or not it is, in actuality, good. Look into the future. What would your life be like if you continued that course of action? Would it be good? Would your life be richer? If you determine that it is something good (though doing it makes you feel bad now), decide to start thinking about it differently—look past the pain of it to the joy of its reward. Then *do* the uncomfortable, hard thing, but do it with joy! Rejigger your emotions and commit to the thing; don't let your feelings set the course of your life. There's a chance you'll end up ruining a lot of things that could have been wonderful if you do.

Consider a troubled marriage. What do you do with that? Ignore it? One of the laws of relationship is: *tension demands attention.* That is certainly not *fun.* And most people feel bad about confronting others on issues that need to be addressed. So they avoid it altogether. There is more joy in avoidance than in confrontation—at least in the beginning. The problem is, couples who avoid confrontation shelve critical issues that must be dealt with. Over time the shelf gets full, and eventually, it breaks.

Bill Hybels writes:

Tenderhearted people will go to unbelievable lengths to avoid any kind of turmoil, unrest or upheaval in a relationship. If there's a little tension in the marriage and one partner asks the other, "What's wrong?" the tender one will answer, "Nothing." What he or she is really saying is this: "Something's wrong, but I don't want to make a scene." In

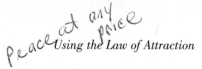
choosing peace keeping over truth telling, these people think they are being noble, but in reality they are making a bad choice. Whatever caused the tension will come back. The peace will get harder and harder to keep. A spirit of disappointment will start to flow through the peace keeper's veins, leading first to anger, then to bitterness and finally to hatred. Relationships can die while everything looks peaceful on the surface!

Peace at any price is a form of deception from the pit of hell. When you know you need to tell the truth, the evil one whispers in your ear, "Don't do it. He won't listen. She won't take it. It will make things worse. It's not worth it." If you believe those lies, there is a high probability that you will kill your relationship sooner or later.[11]

The truth is, confrontation needs to be embraced; it is a key to real intimacy—and that *is* fun.

And what of raising children? I never enjoyed correcting my kids. I am the kind of dad who loved giving them whatever they wanted. But always giving children what they want is a recipe for raising third-world dictators, not responsible adults. Raising kids to responsible adulthood demands that we do some *un*fun things.

Feeling bad about what you're doing doesn't necessitate that you stop. If that was true, why would you do *anything* hard? Why get up and go to work? That's hard sometimes. Or why not go to work and just sit in your office, cut out pictures of what you want, and imagine millions of dollars of bonuses being stuffed in your in-box?

Why study for school? That's no fun. Just feel good feelings and *imagine* getting straight A's on your tests. Why work out at the gym? That's definitely hard. It hurts. Why not just eat salami sandwiches and take naps all day? Just embrace the "feelings" of being fit . . . just "imagine" that you are in great health.

I don't really believe Byrne and her team are saying all *that*, but they are sure not warning against it. Byrne writes, "The most important thing for you to know is that it is impossible to feel bad and at the same time be having good thoughts. When you are feeling bad, you are on the frequency of drawing more bad things. As you feel bad, you are in effect saying, 'Bring me more circumstances that will make me feel bad. Bring it on.'"[12] She continues, "When you are feeling bad, it is communication for the Universe, and in effect it is saying, 'Warning! Change thinking now. Negative frequency recording. Change frequency. Counting down to manifestation. Warning!'"[13]

Life Is Supposed To Be Good

Yes, our thoughts and feelings compose the largest portion of what we call "life," and they create an aura that goes out and draws back to us comparable circumstances. Good thoughts and emotions draw good situations. Bad ones draw bad situations. God gave us life as a gift; it is supposed to be good. Life does not have to be constant drudgery and a struggle. We need to avoid bad thoughts and feelings and embrace good ones in their place. But keep in mind that leaning only

34

toward good feelings can be a cop-out and not an effective use of any of these ideas.

Our thoughts and feelings are mirrored back into our lives—they create the circumstances that surround us. Ever walk into a room where people have been fighting? The air is heavy with darkness. There is a palpable negativity in the room. Contrariwise, what about homes full of respect and love? The air is light and fresh. The rooms are brighter somehow. What is the difference between a home filled with strife and a home filled with affection and respect? Just the thoughts and feelings that people hold for one another.

Remember Churchill's words, "You create your own universe as you go along." We need to master our thoughts and feelings—*they create our reality.* This is not to suggest that God is not to be praised. He is the one responsible for creating these laws to begin with. As we witness the good things that pour into our lives as a result of the law of attraction, we can praise him as exuberantly as the farmer can for a bountiful harvest! Yes, the farmer is the one who, in his own sweat, worked the field—but it is still God who, appropriately, is worthy of all the worship.

Moses challenged the children of Israel on this very point. He said, "If you start thinking to yourselves, 'I did all this. And all by myself. I'm rich. It's all mine!'—well, think again. Remember that GOD, your God, gave you the strength to produce all this wealth so as to confirm the covenant that he promised to your ancestors—as it is today."[14]

4

I've Got a Feeling

Let's talk some more about feelings. If monitoring feelings is critical to utilizing the inherent power of the law of attraction, we need to understand our feelings well. *Think of it:* your feelings are magnets, pulling either good or bad toward your life, your home, your kids, and your relationships. *Dude.* You need to get onto this—*fast.*

But before we dig deeper, let me make a quick, overarching statement. As I have already said, contrary to the assertions made by those who promote the most current usage of the law of attraction, *thoughts and feelings are not the only forces at play in your life.* All things being equal, the law of attraction works, just as the law of sowing and reaping works. However, there are times when they are preempted by the presence of other forces.

For example, every farmer approaches the planting season with the confidence that the law of sowing and reaping is going to work. And in most cases it will. But what if there is a drought or a hurricane or a freeze that season? Crops will fail. The farmer would not

step 1 / The people places & things we are powerless over.

36

then conclude that the law of sowing and reaping no longer works; he would recognize that other forces entered and superseded the law of sowing and reaping.

Consider the law of gravity. It is always present. But how do you account for those powered metal objects flying around in the air? It's not that gravity doesn't affect airplanes; it is that they operate under a different law: the law of lift. On this planet, the law of lift can usurp the law of gravity.

I take issue with the latest usage of the law of attraction because of its supporters' reticence to admit that the law can be set aside by other powers. They never discuss this. On the contrary, they consistently hold to the notion that the law itself is sovereign, there is no force or law that can displace it. If you work this law, they contend, it will succeed every time— no exceptions. But there *are* other forces greater than the law of attraction. Let's take a look.

The Secret and God

God and his will always take precedence over the Secret. You can pretend that he doesn't exist, and "law-of-attraction" yourself away all day, but that doesn't mean things will end as you imagined. Jesus told his followers as much in this story:

> "The farm of a certain rich man produced a terrific crop. He talked to himself: 'What can I do? My barn isn't big enough for this harvest.'

Then he said, 'Here's what I'll do: I'll tear down my barns and build bigger ones. Then I'll gather in all my grain and goods, and I'll say to myself, Self, you've done well! You've got it made and can now retire. Take it easy and have the time of your life!'

"Just then God showed up and said, 'Fool! Tonight you die. And your barnful of goods—who gets it?'

"That's what happens when you fill your barn with Self and not with God."[1]

Consider the Culture

Then there is the force of the vox populi—the mass mind-set of the culture in which we live. I don't care how much you imagine it; you are not going to "law-of-attraction" away the drug problem in America all on your own by thinking "good" thoughts and feeling "good" emotions. Neither will you banish racism and sexism nor fix the plight of the poor by cutting out happy pictures and conjuring up "happy thoughts."

The Problem of Sin

Then there is the force of the *law of sin and death*.[2] This is the law responsible for putting the whole world into a negative trajectory since the Fall in Genesis 3. Yes, God is working to restore that, but that is the work of redemptive grace, which is of a higher order than common grace— where the law of attraction functions. This is why, though we can change much in our lives using the law of attraction, we cannot change *enough*. We cannot "think" ourselves saved; neither can we cultivate enough good feelings to save ourselves—the world still needs a Savior.

The Secret and Satan

Finally, there is the force of the *kingdom of darkness*. Scripture states "that the whole world is under the control of the evil one."[3] Now, *there's* a bad thought! You can try to ignore it. You can try to use the "tricks" espoused by Byrne's team, such as doing your "Secret Shifters"[4]—exercises that shift your mood instantly, like listening to a favorite piece of music, singing, or recalling a great memory or a funny moment—but it will not liberate you from this spiritual bondage.

Paul explains our bleak condition: "At one time you were dead because of your sins. You followed the sinful ways of the world and obeyed the leader of the power of darkness. He is the devil who is now working in the people who do not obey God. At one time all of us lived to please our old selves. We gave in to what our bodies and minds wanted. We were sinful from birth like all other people."[5]

You can't use the law of attraction to get out of mess like this. Jesus had to die to fix it. It cost him his life to break the control of Satan over humankind—he didn't just use some secret idea. As a result of Jesus' amazing love and sacrifice, Scripture reports, "God rescued us from dead-end alleys and dark dungeons. He's set us up in the kingdom of the Son he loves so much, the Son who got us out of the pit we were in."[6]

Breaking Strongholds

I do agree with the Byrne team that we do not want to live our lives feeling bad. I also agree that feeling bad is an indicator that we are thinking bad thoughts. We don't want to do that either. Today's backer of law-of-attraction philosophy believes that if you feel good, then the future that you are consequently creating for yourself will be heading in the same direction as your desires. If you feel bad, then the opposite is true. The things you want and the future you are creating will be on different tracks. And since every imagination and emotion is creating the life ahead of you, then you must be careful not to let negative thinking rule your mind. If you do, then negative outcomes will surely return to you. For example, the more anxiety you feel on a daily basis, the more of that you will bring into your life—every day. (Remember, the law of attraction is at work *at all times*.)

OK. But what I don't agree with is any attempt to deal with bad feelings with a quick fix. For instance, the Byrne team tells us, "When you're feeling down, did you know that you can change it in an instant? Put on a beautiful piece of music, or start singing—that'll change your emotion. Or think of something beautiful. Think of a baby or somebody that you truly love, and dwell on it. Really keep that thought in your mind. Block everything out but that thought. I guarantee you'll start to feel good."[7]

I concur with this assertion in *some* cases (like when the thinker happens to be an emotionally healthy, spiritually mature individual), but honestly I would have to say, in most cases I don't. Since feelings are indicators of what's *really* going on inside us, then moving too quickly to abandon bad ones in an attempt to secure good ones can actually be a form of *denial.* Denial is never a good thing.

Feeling bad has a certain level of complexity to it. You may not immediately understand why you are feeling bad to begin with. We often develop patterns of thinking which cause us to feel bad, and we've been at it for so long that we don't even remember which thoughts originally fostered the pattern. We just live in the bad feeling. Maybe those negative emotions can be traced to a tragic childhood moment. Others may be the result of unforgiveness that we are harboring against someone. A feeling of dread may lurk in the back of our psyches from a past failure, so, whenever we get into a situation similar to the one in which we failed, we instantly start to feel all of those bad feelings again—sometimes without even consciously knowing *why.* Some of us have deep-seated feelings of inferiority or a deeply rooted sense of shame—these things jam our emotions with toxicity.

All of these complex thought patterns can produce crippling, chronic bad feelings. We cannot let them dwell in our souls. Doing so will cause the law of attraction to work to our harm—continually drawing events, circumstances, and feelings that affirm our failure, inferiority, shame, and so on. However, to suggest that we just push these off instantly by singing or eating a salami sandwich or petting the family cat seems a bit silly or, worse, Pollyannaish. This isn't transformation; this is *pretending.* It's denial at its worst.

Biblically, these intrinsic, negative thought patterns that produce bad feelings are called "strongholds,"[8] so named because they "hold" you, and they do so *strongly*. God does not want human beings living in the *land of suck*. He wants us to feel great and to be happy.

Listen to Jesus' words to his apprentices: "Are you tired? Worn out? . . . Come to me. Get away with me and you'll recover your life. I'll show you how to take a real rest. Walk with me and work with me— watch how I do it. Learn the unforced rhythms of grace. I won't lay anything heavy or ill-fitting on you. Keep company with me and you'll learn to live freely and lightly."[9] God promised his people, Israel, while they were still captive to the Babylonian Empire, "I have it all planned out—plans to take care of you, not abandon you, plans to give you the future you hope for."[10]

God promises freedom and a way to help us consistently feel good, but the road to freedom, where strongholds lose their hold, is not by some kind of cheap pretending. We are not supposed to trick our minds into believing we live in wonderland when we are really camping just outside the gates of hell. Our liberty is secured as we take God by the hand and let him lead us on the precarious path of appropriately dealing with the past and joyfully facing the future.

Only the tools that *God* gives "have divine power to demolish strongholds."[11] Step 3 Turning our will & our lives over to God.

Getting in Touch

Those of us who are followers of Jesus are pretty oriented to faith—so much so that we sometimes ignore our feelings. You kind of get in that habit when you love someone you can't see. But ignoring or suppressing

our feelings

our feelings is not a good thing to do. In fact, ignoring them keeps us from being radically transformed by God.

In his book *Emotionally Healthy Spirituality*, Peter Scazzero does a brilliant job discussing the average Christian's aversion to feelings and how it often leads to unresolved anger and frustration. Scazzero claims that many believers are hard to be around because they have not learned how to process the emotions that are present deep within them. Instead of coming to God with our bad feelings and emotions, Scazzero says believers actually use God *to run from God*: "On the surface all appears to be healthy and working, but it's not. All those hours and hours spent lost in one Christian book after another . . . all those many Christian responsibilities outside the home or going from one seminar to another . . . all that extra time in prayer and Bible study. At times we use these Christian activities as an unconscious attempt to escape from pain."[12]

Sensitivity Training

Each of us was created physically with nerves that "warn" us by feeling pain—that's how we know when we've stepped on a nail or have an infection. Here's a wild thought. What if God actually created us to experience bad feelings so we could have built-in indicators of wrong thinking? "Why would he do such a thing?" you might ask. Maybe so we can address the problem and experience healing. It would sure cause us to rethink the negative feelings we encountered. Instead of trying to deny them or run from them, we would be tempted to follow them back to their source, with the hope that God will meet us with healing.

restore us to sanity

Scazzero writes:

Many of us Christians believe wholeheartedly that anger, sadness, and fear are sins to be avoided, indicating something is wrong with our spiritual life. Anger is dangerous and unloving toward others. Sadness indicates a lack of faith in the promises of God; depression surely reveals a life outside the will of God! And fear? The Bible is filled with commands to "not be anxious about anything" and "do not fear" (see Philippians 4:6 and Isaiah 41:10).

So what do we do? We try to inflate ourselves with a false confidence to make those feelings go away. We quote Scripture, pray Scripture, memorize Scripture—anything to keep ourselves from being over-whelmed by those feelings![13]

Feelings, he argues, are often impacted by the sinister voices from our surrounding world and our pasts. They haunt us with deeply held negative beliefs, leading us to believe the following lies:

- I am a mistake.
- I am a burden.
- I am stupid.
- I am worthless.
- I must be approved of by certain people to be OK.
- I don't have the right to experience joy and pleasure.

- I have no right to assert myself or say what I think and feel.
- I have no right to feel good about myself.[14]

Scazzero stresses that we must not bury these feelings but unearth them in God's presence. He says we cannot really listen to what God is saying or evaluate what is going on inside our lives if we ignore the bad feelings. We need to process them, but we should never *ignore* or *suppress* them.

For example, you know you are biblically commanded to love those around you—but say there's this guy that you sort of "love to hate." You refuse to continue fueling your non-love feelings, not by denying them but by processing them. You ask God to help you understand *why* you are having feelings of hate. Perhaps he reminds you of someone who hurt you in the past. You then ask him to help you forgive and to appreciate and love that unlovable guy, just as God does.[15] At first it will feel as though it's "killing" you, but you continue to trust God's hand in your soul to work through the forgiveness and to reprocess your feelings. Eventually you begin to feel love for the guy. The Bible calls this kind of mind-set reorientation, getting your "senses trained."[16]

The Gift of Pain

To review, feelings are indicators of our thoughts. Bad feelings reveal that bad thoughts are going through our heads. Good feelings indicate that good thoughts are going through our heads. We are obviously after good thoughts, because according to the law of attraction, our thoughts and feelings are magnets—drawing like things back to us. So, we don't want bad feelings. But we don't want to be in denial either.

Here's a brainteaser: Should we feel *good* about feeling *bad*? Maybe. Why? Because pain is a gift—it points us to the place where problems lie.

Whenever I go to my doctor with an ache or pain, he asks me, "Where does it hurt?" When I tell him my symptoms, he can diagnose what's going on and recommend a course of action. Pain was the *gift* that revealed there was trouble going on in my body—it was my signal to get some repair. The pain was never really the problem; the problem was the problem. The pain just alerted me *to* the problem—it brought it to my attention.

Emotional Leprosy

Dr. Paul Brand is famous for his work among lepers. Leprosy is one of those diseases that people don't like to talk about. Untreated, leprosy leaves its victims with horrible disfigurement: their noses wither; they lose fingers and toes, then hands and feet; and many go blind.

In his work with lepers, Dr. Brand discovered that it was not the disease of leprosy that caused patients' flesh to deteriorate—at least not directly. Their disfigurement was actually the result of the fact that they did not feel pain. Lepers, it turns out, destroy themselves unwittingly. They step on pieces of glass and don't feel it. They break a toe or scrape off their skin down to the bone without so much as a twinge of sensation.

Brace yourself. The following is a graphic, uncomfortable story:

One day Dr. Brand arrived at one of the leprosariums in India to do a group clinic. His visit had been announced in advance, and when the camp administrators rang the bell to get the patients' attention, a large group of lepers quickly began to move to the area where the clinic was being held.

Dr. Brand noticed that one young patient was trying to beat the rest of them to the tent. At first he struggled across the courtyard, using his crutches and holding his bandaged left leg clear off the ground. But as other patients began to get ahead of him, he decided to race. As Dr. Brand watched, this young guy tucked his crutches under his arm and began running. He ended up near the head of the line, where he stood panting, leaning on his crutches, and sporting a huge smile of triumph.

Dr. Brand knew from the odd way he had been running that something was seriously wrong. Walking toward him to investigate, he saw that his bandages were wet with blood, and his left foot flopped freely from side to side. By running on an already dislocated ankle, he had put far too much force on the end of his leg bone and had ripped away the flesh under the stress. He had no clue that he was running on the end of his tibia bone! As Dr. Brand knelt beside the man, he found that small stones and twigs had jammed through the end of the bone into the marrow cavity. He had no choice but to amputate the leg just below the knee.[17]

OK. Horrible story. But I had to tell it for one reason: to show you that *pain is a gift*, though it's one that most people don't want. But if we try to avoid pain or ignore the bad feelings, we are really setting ourselves up for emotional leprosy, not personal transformation. Bad feelings can reveal secrets about what you believe and how you have wrongly handled the past—which can often correct wrong thinking and lead to new levels of joy and freedom! Don't run through life, avoiding your emotional pain. You'll just hurt yourself worse.

Locate your bad feelings. Bring them to God. Then ask him to help you see what they are indicating, and let him heal you there. Then you will be ready for the law of attraction to work. I love the work that author Rhonda Byrne has done to bring the law of attraction to the forefront for many, but working it isn't as easy as her book suggests— again, *there is more to this Secret . . .*

5

Why Christians
Get Nervous About This

There are already those in Christian circles decrying the validity of Rhonda Byrne's book, *The Secret*. Some are characterizing the recent reemergence of these ideas as "the power of positive thinking meets name-it-and-claim-it theology." Others are saying it is just another round of well-worn blather from the "self-help gurus," which is definitely neither new *nor* a secret. Astute theologians and philosophers are quick to point out that this latest iteration of the law of attraction has been repackaged in ancient Gnostic form—as *secret knowledge for the enlightened elite*, whose only consideration for the world's hurting and disenfranchised is to tell them to discover it for themselves.

I agree that there are problems, as I have already been pointing out. Yet dwelling so much on the problem areas could lead us to dismiss the ideas altogether, and that, in my opinion, would be a costly mistake. True, if one cares to, he or she could drown in four inches of water, but why do so? It doesn't take much energy to simply pick up your head and avoid drowning. We Christians need to address the dangers inherent in *any* philosophy, but we can do so without immersing our faces into its problems until we "drown"—thus missing truth that will help people. The ideas in *The Secret* are helping people—even those of us who are already Christ-followers.

There Are Always Imperfections

It could be argued that there is nothing on this planet that has not suffered some degree of corruption since the Fall. We shouldn't be surprised when we run into inconsistencies or untenable aspects in the ideas that we encounter. The majority of the New Testament was written to address imperfections in the lives of the early saints—and after pastoring for more than twenty-five years, I've noticed that there are *still* a few imperfections lingering around.

Did you know that the U.S. Department of Health publishes a booklet entitled *The Food Defect Action Levels*, in which they list specifications of "current levels for natural or unavoidable defects" for chocolate in the form of "insect, rodent, and other natural contaminants" allowed by the FDA? Tolerance levels for chocolate are up to 120 insect fragments or 2 rodent hairs per 8-ounce cup.[1] That means the chocolate bar you eat may contain 1 rodent hair and 16 insect parts, and still carry the FDA's blessing!

You may never eat chocolate again after reading this, but I am undeterred. I still love chocolate. In fact, it is one of my favorite foods. The good of the chocolate outweighs the bad of the hair and bugs.

This also plays into my feeling about the latest renditions of the law of attraction. When I watched *The Secret* DVD and read the book, I had obvious concerns. But I also knew that there was something *right* about what was presented, something profoundly encouraging and strengthening. The whole idea that we don't have to stay stuck and bound by our circumstances; the hope that life can be sweeter and that we can smile at the future; the idea that dark thoughts and feelings can be usurped by good ones—all of it rumored the kingdom of God for me.

However, there were parts of the presentation that seemed to have more rodent hair and insect parts than I was able to swallow (hence, this book). But on the whole, I think the inherent good of this "chocolate" far outweighs the bad. Unfolding the law of attraction for this generation is going to bring much good fruit. Instead of recoiling, I believe the Church needs to recognize and utilize the power inherent in this law. We need to become experts at employing this ancient practice.

My Favorite Parts

There are a number of "high water" marks about the law of attraction that, if the Church would heed, could help us advance the cause of Christ in the world. (These are the insect- and rodent-free parts!)

The Schema

I think using the law of attraction to explain why our thoughts and feelings matter is brilliant. It says to me that God has given us gifts that can be used to change the quality of our lives. It implies that we need to be more intentional about what is going on between our ears. It suggests that people don't have to be victims. And it means that we can chart our course and purpose to experience more of the abundance and good that God has placed in this world.

I love the idea that each of us can *intentionally* think good thoughts—that our imaginations are not unalterable because they are just "who we are." No! We can choose thoughts of health, provision, peace, forgiveness, and strong relationships—and somehow when we think this way, our thoughts "run out" (are transmitted) and grab those things that we are thinking about, bringing the "fruit" of those thoughts back to us!

The field of neuroscience has proven that thoughts emit differing magnetic frequencies within the cerebral cortex—frequencies that can be mapped using equipment like a magnetic resonance imaging (MRI) machine. The claim that thoughts have "frequencies," made by modern interpretations of the law of attraction, is empirically verifiable.

However, whether or not these frequencies are "broadcast" to the wider world in order to attract "like" things back to the agent broadcasting those frequencies is a hypothesis—there is no empirical data available to prove it. *So what?* I know this may sound a little whacky to some, a little "New Agey" at first, but new ideas usually hit us as strange. We may not know exactly how this works, but there *is something working.* And we shouldn't be afraid to imagine what it might be for fear that we are treading on ground that belongs only to God (we'll come back to this).

Nervous Saints

I think we church folk are way too fidgety about new ideas. We always have been. Remember Copernicus, the guy who suggested that the sun didn't revolve around the earth, but the earth rotated around the sun? That may seem like no biggie to us now, but back in the day, Copernicus's work contradicted then-accepted religious dogma: the Church held that the sun rose and set orbiting around the earth. Further, planet Earth was the center of the solar system—and *they had the Bible verses to prove it!*

Pamphlets were actually produced protesting Copernicus's new ideas as heresy, because Christians believed that his work was destroying faith in God. But that was not true. Science and faith don't have to disrupt each other. It may take some time for us to sort through new scientific data and locate its congruence within the faith paradigm, but true faith and true science always find a way to live in harmony—after all, God made them both. Sadly, it's usually Christians who create confusion and get all nervous about new theories.

It wasn't long ago that people believed disease was "spontaneously generated," either by God (or the gods), devils, or personal sin. In the mid-fourteenth century, as the bubonic plague (the Black Death) ravaged Europe, there were those who thought it was the judgment of God (like those TV preachers in the early 1980s who claimed that AIDS was God's judgment on homosexuals).

But then came the germ theory—the belief that disease is caused by microscopic germs—a fairly recent discovery (mid 1800s). At first, the idea that disease was being created by microorganisms, which grow by reproduction rather than unseen forces managed by God, was met with steep resistance.

During the nineteenth century, women in childbirth were dying at alarming rates in Europe and the United States. Up to 25 percent of women who delivered their babies in hospitals died from what was called "childbed fever." In the late 1840s, Dr. Ignaz Semmelweis, who worked in the maternity wards of a Vienna hospital, observed that the mortality rate in a delivery room staffed by medical students was up to three times higher than in a second delivery room, staffed by midwives. In fact, the midwives were terrified of the room staffed by the med students. Dr. Semmelweis noticed that the students were coming directly to the delivery room from their lessons in the autopsy room. He postulated that the students might be carrying the infection from their dissections to birthing mothers. So he ordered doctors and medical students to wash their hands with a chlorinated solution before examining women in labor. This was a completely new idea! When the students followed through, the mortality rate in his maternity wards dropped from 25 percent to less than 1 percent!

Despite the remarkable results, Semmelweis's colleagues greeted his findings with hostility. It was too fantastical. Too ridiculous. Kind of voodooish. (New Agey?) Some actually believed that trying to "fix" the mortality problem among mothers and babies was an intrusion into God's sovereignty—that such things needed to be left in the hands of God.

Dr. Semmelwies eventually resigned his position. Later, he had similar dramatic results with hand washing in another maternity clinic but to no avail. When he died in 1865, his views were still largely ridiculed. Why? Humans tend to ridicule *any* new way of looking at things, probably because we feel threatened. Embracing the new idea proves that we were *not* thinking right before—that we have, in fact, been wrong (God forbid!). We have much too much hubris in us (insect and rodent parts) for that. This is especially true for those of us in the church.

Not only do church folk carry opinions, but we find Bible passages to prove that God is siding with us—we love to "swear by heaven"[2] This habit continues for those in the church who have rashly rejected these latest books in traditional, hotheaded fashion.

What if It's True?

The overarching schema espoused by the proponents of this so-called "secret"—that my thoughts are actually going out, grabbing what's like them, and pulling it back into my life—is so vivid, so graphic, so easy to get one's mind around. It carries an inherent warning about entertaining bad and evil in one's mind, along with a hopeful course of action to encourage the positive and the hopeful.

This schema makes me want to work at thinking right about things, to pay more attention to my feelings to ensure I am on track. This framework helps me understand *why* the Bible speaks so strongly and so frequently about believers' thought lives. This is the reason why "as a person thinks, so will his or her life be."[3]

And I don't think this takes anything away from the domain or rule of God in our lives. God is still the one who created all the provision in the universe and who provides the joy and health and whatever else you can imagine. He is the Provider, the Strengthener, the Healer, the Helper, the Hope Giver. This secret—the way of looking at what's going on—simply gives us more access to what God has created—it doesn't replace God any more than a farmer who has learned to work the law of sowing and reaping can replace God.

This scheme doesn't eliminate God (or the devil). In fact, the law of attraction may prove to be the *very way*—the anatomy of—how the will of God (or the negative plan of the devil) is actually accomplished through our lives. When we understand the Secret, it encourages us to be good stewards of our thoughts and emotions!

If This Was True, I Would Know It Already

We profess to be Bible people, and we claim to believe the Bible. Thus, it's easy to reason, "If this law is really true, why would we Christians need someone who isn't quoting Scripture (or even a Christian him- or herself) to tell *us* about it?" Good question. Allow me to recall something I wrote in my book *Religiously Transmitted Diseases* that might shed some light on it.

A *hermeneutic* is a method or principle that we use to interpret truth. We all have a hermeneutic. It helps us determine the meaning of what is going on around us. For example, in the premodern world, a violent natural event, like an earthquake or an exploding volcano, was thought to be some kind of vengeance from the gods. That was a hermeneutic to the people of that time. Gods do that sort of thing. So whenever there was a natural disaster, people assumed that someone had killed a sacred animal or committed some heinous crime that angered the gods. The cataclysm was retribution for that immoral act.

In the modern world, we know that natural disasters brew because of a number of very natural conditions. That is *our* hermeneutic. What premoderns saw as acts of the gods, moderns see as the logical result of nature's adjustments. No vengeance here.

A different hermeneutic leads to a different interpretation.

The hermeneutics we use provide a framework for processing data, as prescription eyeglasses "frame" what we (who need them) see. I remember getting my first pair of glasses as a kid and being amazed at how they helped me see the world in a whole new way—clearly. I had become used to the blur.

In my small hometown in rural Wisconsin, I knew a lady who believed that there was no way the United States ever got those men on the moon—not really. When asked about the live television broadcasts that captured the event, she would say, "It was all Hollywood. They staged the whole thing. It was fake, and a bunch of people made a lot of money from our tax dollars." Her hermeneutic "glasses" made the whole thing appear as a hoax. She lived with a "conspiracy" hermeneutic.

Sadly, Christians fail to recognize that we all come to the Bible with presuppositions (hermeneutics) that impact the way the Bible reads to us. All kinds of things influence us: our experiences, our parents, Dr. Phil, our friends, the churches we've attended, *The Matrix*, our prejudices, expectations, hopes, failures, God, the devil, being American, an *Oprah* show we once saw—these all color the way we interpret our world and our faith. They color our hermeneutic.

Tattoos and Body Piercing

Let's say that you grew up believing that it is wrong for people to get tattoos and have their body pierced. Maybe you heard your mom and dad say it was wrong. Or perhaps it's because when you were growing up, tattoos and body piercing were only fashionable for mean-looking bikers, biker chicks, and those on the shallow end of the socioeconomic scale. Is that an unfair prejudice? Absolutely. But if that was your experience, it impacts how you think.

Whatever the reason, inbred opinions cause us to read Bible texts with a predetermined selectivity—some texts literally pop off the page at us, while others remain completely ignored.

We may come across the verse, "Do not cut your bodies . . . or put tattoo marks on yourselves" (Lev. 19:28), and it leaps off the page. And when an internal "resonance" occurs, it can feel very much like a spiritual epiphany—like the voice of God. *No wonder tattoos and pierced noses trouble us so,* we reason. *God feels the same way!*

Never mind that in the previous verse men are told to never "cut the hair at the sides of your head or clip off the edges of your beard" (v. 27). We ignore that. But if we choose to obey the command that forbids tattoos or piercings on the basis of God's Word, then we must by necessity of reason demand that men grow side-mullets and sport scraggly, untrimmed beards—with a great big "Praise the Lord!"

So, why aren't we fair and reasonable with Bible texts like these? Because something in us longs to emphasize those verses that resonate with our own opinions and biases, while ignoring the ones that don't. It's one thing to interpret matters in a biased way, but it's quite another to slap *God's* endorsement on our interpretation. But people do it every day.

This is why we have to be open to truth that comes to us from outside the normal context—like a casual reading of the Bible. It isn't that the Bible doesn't address everything we need to know—I believe it does. But we tend to only see *selectively*, and though we may have the truth right in front of our eyes, we don't always catch it.

How many times, while reading the Bible, have you thought, *I never saw* that *before*? Chances are there's more you haven't seen. Be open.

Devil Worshippers Wear Shoes Too

Being "open" means that we have to stop being afraid of lateral thinking (thinking outside of the box). We must be willing to reimagine how things work in God's world. We have to quit falling prey to the fearmongers who claim that everything foreign to our current way of thinking must be of the devil.

So many of the jewels of the past have been lost by the church simply because they were strange to us, by virtue of the culture in which we grew up. For instance, meditation was widely practiced in the early church, but until very recently, modern Christian leaders warned against it. The argument opposing it usually stated that people of "other" faiths—faiths filled with deception—participate in meditation. I have heard preachers say passionately, "Even devil worshippers do it!"

When the average pew-sitter hears those words, there is a general panic. And any new thoughts are effectively quelled. It turns out that the church has its own version of McCarthyism, and it is fairly easy to target ideas and create such an atmosphere of suspicion that people stop thinking critically and simply give credence to the suspicions they hear, despite the inconclusive evidence offered.

But these kinds of arguments just don't make sense. The pagan religious and the devil worshippers also eat and sleep. Why don't we stop doing those things as well as stay away from meditation? Devil worshippers wear clothes and shake hands when they greet one another—are those things wrong too?

And need I mention the money and power that fear making garners? Overreactionary, fear-generating purveyors of woe and danger make their livings causing church people to panic and are experts at getting folks to keep coming back to them for more. (No one wants to miss finding out what might hurt them if they don't know about it!)

It reminds me of Chicken Little, when he warned, "The sky is falling!" His kind of overreacting always yields quite a stir, fear is contagious. Chicken Little always seems to meet up with Henny Penny, Cocky Locky, and Goosey Poosey, and then you really have a mess. It turns into a whole fear movement.

So . . .

Here's my point: just because an idea is new to us doesn't mean it is wrong—nor does it mean that all that is said about it is right either. We should never be uncritical of truth, but we do need to chill out a little, or we will run the risk of missing truths that could help us live more fruitful, transformed lives.

Next, let's look at another enterprise presented by modern interpreters of the law of attraction—something that is usually perceived as scary by modern evangelicals—*visualization.*

Buckle up, Harold. There are a few more unsettling notions to consider . . .

6

How Christians Should
Use the Law of Attraction

Just for the record, I do not believe our purpose in life should be to secure as much wealth, health, and fame as we can possibly get our greedy little fingers around. It seems to me that even a casual perusal of Scripture reveals that a life of having everything you want is a small life indeed. Just read Ecclesiastes, or take a look at the temptation of Jesus in the wilderness. He was offered the "kingdoms of the world" and decided to pass.[1] What was he thinking? As his apprentice, I have made it my goal to find out.

Yet, the majority of the material you run into on the subject of the law of attraction is not about using it for anything altruistic or for the good of others. Instead, the information is often about giving individual users all the fitness, fortune, and fame they could ever imagine. Most of the literature you encounter also makes hefty promises for those who learn to use this law—promises such as these:

- You'll discover the secret to having anything you want in life, and you'll know exactly how to get it.

- Your self-esteem and confidence will soar.

- You'll discover the key to peace of mind and freedom from fear, doubt, and worry.

- You'll be happy and fulfilled.

- You can choose whatever you want; it doesn't matter how big it is.

- You'll discover the recipe for personal and financial freedom.

- You'll finally understand why everything always seems to work out for some people, while others never seem to catch a break.

- You'll become the master of your destiny and learn how to create the future you desire and deserve.

- You can eliminate your financial problems and have all the money you wish for.

- You'll learn how to create "dreams on demand" and thus create your future.

- You'll discover the secret to having endless energy and enthusiasm for each new day.

- You'll break free from limiting beliefs and obstacles that hold you back from having what you want in life.

- You can have, do, and be absolutely everything you want in life.
- You'll feel like a brand-new person, living each day with joy, excitement, and anticipation of all the good things headed your way.

Such New Age resources promise to show you how to use the law of attraction (getting control of your thought life, managing your emotions, using visualization, etc.) with the goal of giving you a "picture-perfect life." You are taught how to replace mental pictures that "no longer serve you," and how to "cast off" the old and "unlock" the incredible power that's "in you" to move forward in your life (which means learning how to think of yourself as "wealthy and successful" all the time). You are told to think thoughts and feel feelings that help to create a "vivid vision"—the life you "truly desire and deserve."

People are encouraged to take the time to write a very detailed description of what they want their lives to be like in every area, and to cut out pictures of things they would like to own—cars, homes, businesses, *whatever*. Armed with these new visions, they are told to spend a few minutes every day visualizing that they already have the things they want to have. They are to feel the feelings they would if they had their dream property in their possession now—they are to conjure up feelings of gratitude and excitement in the present tense. This, they are told, is how to best utilize the power behind the law of attraction. This is how you can *have*, *be*, or *do* anything *without limits*.

The materials assure you that you will be able to have all the success, happiness, fulfillment, and abundance that you can handle—and it all comes quickly and easily—sometimes with a money-back guarantee. It is the world of 1-800-GET-WHATEVER-YOU-WANT-AND-GET-IT-QUICK. (And you won't want to wait *another minute* to call.)

There is nothing in these popular materials quite so ominous and radical as Jesus' talk about "losing your life" or "taking up your cross."[2] Not hardly.

There Is a Better Way

Because of the way the law of attraction (in all its various iterations) has been used to entice and engender the *lust for more*, it tends to violate the sensibilities of the serious followers of Jesus. And rightly so. Scripture doesn't applaud a life committed to selfdom. Christ-followers don't see their role as the gatherers of *more stuff.* In fact, there is a general sense that "stuff-gathering" is a waste of precious time and is contrary to our core mission here on planet Earth.

We agree with the witness of the Bible guys and gals. People like Solomon, who cried out, "I denied myself nothing my eyes desired; I refused my heart no pleasure." Yet, in the end he asserted, "Everything was meaningless, a chasing after the wind; nothing was gained under the sun."[3]

Then there's Abraham and Sarah. They were actually extremely wealthy (and God was the one who claimed responsibility for it), but they never lived lives committed to gathering *more.* Instead of building large houses or enormous mansions (like the ones in Egypt and Babylon, with which they were familiar), they chose to live simply—wandering around in tents—presumably nice ones, but they were still *tents.* The Scripture says they did this on purpose because they realized "that they were aliens and strangers on earth."[4]

Now, there's a radical idea: Abraham and Sarah saw the earth, in its current state, as *foreign soil.* They didn't think there was anything here worth committing their lives to. "Instead," the Scripture continues, "they were longing for a better country—a heavenly one. Therefore God is not ashamed to be called their God, for he has prepared a city for them."[5]

David asked God to keep him safe from people who loved this world too much: "O LORD, by your hand save me from such men, from men of this world whose reward is in this life."[6] The apostle John warned, "Don't love the world's goods. Love of the world squeezes out love for the Father. Practically everything that goes on in the world—wanting your own way, wanting everything for yourself, wanting to appear important—has nothing to do with the Father. It just isolates you from him. The world and all its wanting, wanting, wanting is on the way out—but whoever does what God wants is set for eternity."[7]

Then there is Moe (or Moses, for those of you who prefer proper names). Here's a guy with it all. He is on the ruling court at the hippest place on earth—this is the LA of the ancient world—glorious Egypt. And Moses is a celebrity. But he chucks it all. Scripture says, "By faith, Moses, when grown, refused the privileges of the Egyptian royal house. He chose a hard life with God's people rather than an opportunistic soft life of sin with the oppressors. He valued suffering in the Messiah's camp far greater than Egyptian wealth because he was looking ahead, anticipating the payoff. By an act of faith, he turned his heel on Egypt . . . He had his eye on the One no eye can see, and kept right on going."[8]

Finally, there is Jesus himself. He claims that he "did not come to be served, but to serve, and to give his life as a ransom for many."[9] He had an "others" orientation, not a selfish, I'm-here-to-grab-all-the-marbles-I-can orientation. Crudely stated, Jesus' position was that a life lived for more is a life wasted.

A Law Is Still a Law

Though we recoil at how the law of attraction is used shamelessly for self-aggrandizement, that doesn't mean it is invalid. The law of attraction still functions, whether you understand and agree with it or not. I appreciate that the negatives associated with the latest books have caused many in the church to discount them. But I think we need to reassess our position. To ignore it would be foolish—bad stewardship. Remember, God is the author of *all* the laws in the universe.

We need to understand, embrace, and utilize the principles of these ideas: we need to remember the importance of thoughts and feelings and the amazing power of visualization. I believe Christians need to use the law of attraction for advancing God's cause in the world.

We live in a culture that has lost track of values beyond what works for personal wants (utilitarianism). Christ-followers must overcome this. We must have goals beyond immediate satisfactions. It's obvious that the law of attraction works for getting what you want—there is way too much anecdotal evidence to discount it. But I think believers need to learn how to use this law for "wants" greater than just selfish ones. We should avoid using it for our own self-interests. We should use the law of attraction in our quest for the administration of God's will and goodness to a hurting world.

A Better Way

The Christian must long for a better world. We say no to using the law *selfishly*. But our "no" is not an end in itself. It implies a "yes" to something more. We say yes to using it to put love where it is not in the world. We are not selfish, because our lives are grounded in values bigger than our solitary needs, desires, and exaggerated sense of fairness and justice. We learn to use these ideas to advance the kingdom of God.

That doesn't mean you can never use the law of attraction to get stuff for yourself—you can. But my challenge would be to always ask yourself *why?* Are you just after stuff in order to keep up with the Joneses? Are you after things because you believe that you are what you have? Is it a self-esteem thing? Do you want *more* as a commitment to a life of ease? Or are you using the law of attraction to have what you need in order to change the world for God?

There is nothing wrong with things, and God *is* our Provider,[10] but there's more to this than just new cars, lakeside homes, and big boats. The late Pope John Paul II said it best: "It is not wrong to want to live better; what is wrong is a style of life which is presumed to be better when it is directed toward 'having' rather than 'being' and which wants to have more not in order to be more, but in order to spend life in enjoyment as an end in itself."[11]

We must develop a self-mastery and discernment that give us the potential to hold on to the right thoughts, feelings, and visualizations needed to carry out a mission beyond self-fulfillment. We need to transform the energy we have devoted to being keepers of things for *ourselves,* to being keepers of hope for those without hope.

The Power of Visualization—What Is It?

Visualization is basically the practice of holding images in your mind of the things you want to have or experience in life. Visualizing the things you want kicks the law of attraction into high gear. However this law works, what goes on in the human mind *attracts* the object of one's imagination to oneself, thereby effectively *creating a new reality* around the one who is doing the imagining. Somehow our thoughts, feelings, and imaginings give concrete shape and substance to our future.

It is at this point that most of the literature dealing with the law of attraction goes consumeristic: *Imagine that new car. See yourself owning that business. Envision a multimillion-dollar house.* The teachers will tell you, "The law of attraction gives you anything you want. It always works—every time, with every person." And they are always talking about *more, more, more* for the big No. 1—you. Because of the directionality of this chatter, I always seem to taste a little "throw-up" in the back of my throat whenever I read it.

However, visualization is still one of the most powerful ways to set your thoughts and feelings down the path drawing in a new future. And believe it or not, visualization is peppered all over the Scriptures.

Visualization in the Bible

Consider the Tower of Babel. Now, here's a feisty group of self-promoters. But notice what God says about them: "Now nothing they have imagined they can do will be impossible for them."[12] This is almighty God's assessment, and he said it about human beings! Visualization is powerful.

Then there is the miracle of provision experienced by Jacob. The story from Genesis 30 is too lengthy to review here, but suffice it to say, Jacob had agreed to work for his father-in-law, with goats and sheep as payment. But Jacob agreed to keep as payment only the animals that were born colored with spots or streaks.

But Laban, Jacob's crafty father-in-law, took all the spotted and streaked goats and all the dark-colored sheep away from Jacob's herd— for those of you not schooled in agrarian genetics, that meant it was *impossible* for Jacob to ever get paid. Laban was a punk. He took all the animals genetically predisposed to color out of the herd.

So how did Jacob respond? Though I am certain he had no idea what he was doing, he used the power of visualization. The Scripture says, "Jacob . . . took fresh-cut branches from poplar, almond and plane trees and made white stripes on them by peeling the bark and exposing the white inner wood of the branches."[13] He then placed those peeled branches directly in front of the place where the flocks mated. As a result of Jacob's visualization, his flock "bore young that were streaked or speckled or spotted."[14] What was impossible became possible through the vehicle of visualization.

In Acts 2, God promises to pour out his Spirit into the world. He says the result will be people who "see visions" and "dream dreams."[15] The Holy Spirit uses visualization to speak into our lives. Though we would be foolish to march into the enterprise of thoughts, feelings, and visualizations without the guidance of the Holy Spirit and the wisdom afforded us in the Word of God, visualization is not of the devil.

As uncomfortable as I have been with admitting that there is something to focusing and thinking and imagining things, there really is truth to it. And if we want to do what we can for the cause of Christ, we need to muster all the things at our disposal to that end. Christians should be really good at using the so-called *secret*.

At one point, when the prophet Isaiah is speaking for God, he declares, "Forget the former things; do not dwell on the past. See, I am doing a new thing! Now it springs up; do you not perceive it?"[16]

God has always wanted his people to "perceive," or envision, what he was about to do—that's visualization. In fact, all the promises of God are invitations for us to perceive or visualize them.

The Book of Imagination

Think of what could happen if we saw all the promises of God as invitations to imagine what could be? Instead of cutting out pictures of BMWs or million-dollar houses to hang on our refrigerators, we could tape up promises that help us imagine a better world: a world that is "filled with the knowledge of the glory of the LORD, as the waters cover the sea."[17] Picture a world where the church is "salt" and "light,"[18] meaning we make life a little tastier for people, and our presence eliminates rot and dispels darkness. Envision a world where believers fearlessly contend against evil and make no peace with oppression; a world where the church consistently uses its freedom to maintain justice in our communities and among the nations; a world where believers imagine themselves to be (as our Savior Jesus was) those who come not to be served but to serve, and by following in his steps we have the wisdom, patience, and courage to minister in his name to the suffering, the friendless, and the needy. *Imagine that.*

Imagine if we used the power of visualization and the law of attraction as we came to God in prayer. What could happen then? Maybe this is what Jesus was getting at when he said, "Whatever you ask for in prayer, believe that you have received it, and it will be yours."[19]

Maybe Jesus was daring us to actually "believe" that when we prayed, it was ours—to actually *imagine* it!

This would mean we could ask God to help us imagine world peace. We could ask him to "kindle in every heart the true love of peace, and guide with your wisdom those who take counsel for the nations of the earth, that in tranquility your dominion may increase until the earth is filled with the knowledge of your love; through Jesus Christ our Lord."[20] *Imagine that.*

Imagine a world free from hunger and prejudice; a world where we see the fulfillment of God's promise, "I will pour out my Spirit on all people."[21] Imagine the nations coming to God in worldwide revival and the fulfillment of the promise in the Psalms, "Ask of me, and I will make the nations your inheritance, the ends of the earth your possession."[22] What if we asked and actually imagined an answer?

What if Paul wasn't kidding when he declared that God "is able to do immeasurably more than all we ask *or imagine*"?[23] What if we dared imagine more? What if we took the thoughts of God—his promises and hope for the world—into *our* minds (vis-à-vis the Scriptures) and opened up our souls to the Holy Spirit for him to impart God's "fruit" into us—his feelings of love, joy, peace, patience, kindness, goodness, faithfulness, gentleness, and self-control? *Imagine that!*

What if God gave us biblical prophecy, not so we could hold the daily news in one hand and the Bible in the other—carefully reading the *New York Times* and the *Jerusalem Post* the way a psychic reads tea leaves, in order to find timelines for the fulfillment of Bible prophecy—but to give us a "snapshot" of the future he intends to give his people? What if he wanted us to have a snapshot so we could cultivate a vision of what the future is going to be—of what the world will be like? The Bible promises that a day is coming when "the dwelling of God" will be with people, "and he will live with them." It claims that we "will be his people, and God himself will be with [us] and be [our] God." Then there's this promise: "He will wipe every tear from [our] eyes. There will be no more death or mourning or crying or pain, for the old order of things has passed away."[24]

What if we imagined a world where God always dwells with us and where all tears are wiped away and all weeping and sorrow are gone? What if we are to carry *that* vision in our minds? Would the law of attraction work to bring us that future more into our now?

Theologians tell us that there is an "eschatological tension" in the kingdom of God—that in one sense the kingdom of God is *here*, but in another sense, *not yet*. Jesus told us, "The kingdom of God is at hand,"[25] yet spoke of it as coming in the future. It's on a continuum somewhere between "here" and "not yet." And apparently believers have something to do with where it is. Jesus told us to pray to the Father, asking, "Thy kingdom come, Thy will be done *in earth, as it is in heaven.*"[26]

However much of the kingdom we experience here, we know we will never *fully* have it until Jesus returns. But the kingdom is among us in some measure, and it can be experienced here now, at least like the measles—in spots. What if we used the law of attraction and our faith to attract more of it into our here and now?

If we thought this way, when we encountered the tears and lament and suffering so present in this fallen world, we would move toward it, bringing with us the hope of the eternal vision. Isn't that what ministry is supposed to be?

Perhaps this is what the writer of Hebrews was referring to when he wrote that the follower of Jesus could partake of "the powers of the coming age."[27] It is with these thoughts in mind that *The Book of Common Prayer* leads us to pray, "Give to us the peace and unity of that heavenly City."[28]

The Bible is clear that the promises of God don't just happen. We are not just to sit back and wait for sovereignty to change the world; we are not to be "lazy," but we are to "imitate those who through faith and patience inherit what has been promised."[29]

I'm suggesting that those of us in the church need to use the power of visualization and the law of attraction for the glory of God and the advancement of his kingdom—not just for health, wealth, success, fulfillment, and personal happiness. *There's more!* Forget about using it to advance consumerism; let's use it to see his kingdom come!

7

The Law of Attraction and Money

We need to talk about money. Though, as believers, we should avoid using these concepts for our own self-interests, we still need to use the law of attraction to secure financial provision for our lives. If we are living in constant scarcity ourselves (riddled with debt or unable to provide basic necessities for our families), we will spend most of our energies and resources surviving and none of them helping others in need. Jesus said, "It is more blessed to give than to receive."[1] Though there may be many reasons why that is true, one reason is because you have it to give.

Money Is Not Evil

Many of the rich people whose stories are sprinkled throughout the Bible credited God for their wealth. Once, Abraham told someone trying to give him a reward, "I will accept nothing belonging to you, not even a thread or the thong of a sandal, so that you will never be able to say, 'I made Abram rich.'"[2] He knew his wealth was the result of

God's blessing. But, as we pointed out, Abraham did not think the wealth was just for *him*.

God said to Solomon, the richest king in Israel's history, "Since you have asked for [wisdom] and not for long life or wealth . . . I will give you what you have not asked for—both riches and honor—so that in your lifetime you will have no equal among kings."[3] This guy used to stack silver in the streets, because it was basically worthless compared to the amount of gold in his possession. When buying from other nations, Israel used silver but demanded gold for its own sales. Later, Jesus used Solomon as the model when he talked about the Father providing for the needs of his followers![4] God made wealth and isn't squeamish about us having some, as long as it is not the focus of our lives (it's both an idol-worship issue and a faith issue, but there's no time to explain here).

We could mention Job—the Bill Gates of his day. Then there were the rich women who supported Jesus' ministry.[5] Jesus had such a habit of giving money away that when Judas went out to betray Jesus, the disciples assumed that Judas was just going out to give more money to the poor.[6] Jesus did this even though he was also responsible for feeding the families of the apostles (twelve families!). Jesus had access to wealth but still led a simple life so he could help more than himself.

Wealth is *not* the problem. But our attitudes, beliefs, and approaches to wealth *can* become problematic. For the believer, acquiring wealth can never be our primary concern, but it is a concern. Paul said the believer "must work, doing something useful with his own hands,"[7] but the reason why is completely different than it is for one who has no faith. He says our motive for gaining wealth should be "that he may have something to share with those in need."[8] Certainly, this would include our families, but not *just* our families. The point of abundance is to be in a position in which we can respond to the needs of *others* in the world.

Scarcity Thinking

You don't have to go very deep into Scripture to discover that God loves to lavishly provide for his creation. The Garden of Eden was a place of abundance. There was a plenitude of food and other natural resources, and it was even said, "The gold of that land is good."[9] And consider the description given at the end of the Bible of the main street of our home on future earth: "The great street of the city was of pure gold, like transparent glass."[10]

God loves gold. He loves nice things. He was the one who made the physical world, with all its wealth, and called it *all* "good."[11] Though we should not make "getting stuff" job #1, God *did* design this planet to bring forth good and abundance for all of us! There are enough resources on the planet for *everyone* in *every* nation to have *every* physical need met in their lives. There is no reason for poverty, homelessness, and deprivation to exist on planet Earth.

But the fundamental axiom of economics in a fallen world is that there is and always will be scarcity. It is based on the fact that we are always waking up and needing more. The stuff we used yesterday is gone. And sometimes it's hard to find more of what we need.

Because of this universal experience, conventional wisdom has always warned that as populations and economies grow, resources will be depleted until, finally, the physical limits are reached and resources are exhausted. Seems like a reasonable claim. After all, if resources are scarce, it stands to reason that increased demand for them will speed up the day when they will disappear from the planet. *Right?*

ENTER: The Prophets of Doom

Hence, warnings of impending catastrophe have always been around. But these warnings rose with increasing fury during the later half of the twentieth century. The population explosion in the developing world, coupled with the dramatic postwar growth of the global economy since 1950, caused economic and scientific prophets of doom to raise the volume, pitch, and urgency of their voices. We were told that civilization was living on "borrowed time." For my generation, the gasoline lines and inflation of the 1970s gave credence to those prophetic voices. International best sellers, such as Paul Ehrlich's *The Population Bomb* and the Carter administration's Global 2000 Report, all helped convince millions of people that civilization as we know it was on the verge of collapse.

Maybe God Didn't Get the Memo

What most folks don't realize is that all the chatter about scarcity is an affront to God's nature, omniscience, and creative power. The Genesis account states, "God blessed them and said to them, 'Be fruitful and increase in number; fill the earth.'"[12] He gave us no warning about population control, nor was he skittish about the strain the commanded growth might put on the planet's resources.

The scarcity mind-set is rooted in the thought, *I'm running out of stuff. What do I do if I don't have enough for tomorrow?* But God's method of provision was always to make sure *today* was taken care of. He never promised us enough to hoard. In fact, God hates hoarding. When he was leading the Israelites through the wilderness, he made sure they had enough bread for *each day*. But some, concerned that they might not have enough, decided to hoard more than they needed. When they did, the Scripture says it became "full of maggots and began to smell."[13]

God isn't interested in eliminating the anxiety we feel when we notice our supplies are running out. We would prefer to have a big old depot we could run out to, full of everything we could ever need, whenever we notice *lack* in our lives. We don't want to have to pay attention to seasons of opportunity so that we find congruence with the rhythm of *supply*. Neither are we eager to learn how to work and cooperate with the laws of attraction/sowing and reaping. We just want a storehouse, preferably close by and already paid for.

And we don't want to share what we do have. Actually, scarcity thinking protects our fallen, selfish natures—if there is a limited supply, it justifies *not sharing*. If there is an unlimited supply, there is no justification for not sharing—there's enough for everyone. We would confidently share what we have as well as corporately engage in the process of locating and gathering more from the abundant world. Teaching others how to do this along with us wouldn't threaten us either—*their* increase won't hurt us in the least. Perhaps God's call for us to share is rooted in the knowledge that there are more than enough resources to go around. We just need to stay diligent and on our toes, using the laws he has given us—laws that lead to abundance.

I even believe that God *wants* the I'm-not-sure-about-tomorrow insecurity in the mix. Jesus told his followers, "Do not worry, saying, 'What shall we eat?' or 'What shall we drink?' or 'What shall we wear?'"[14]

"Do not worry about tomorrow," he continued, "for tomorrow will worry about itself."[15] God wants humans to spin the insecurity about the future into *faith*—not eliminate that insecurity through hoarding.

But provision faith is not just faith in God's doing financial miracles for you and me. He does do those, but I think provision faith is believing that God is *good* enough and *big* enough to provide for every person living on this planet. God is benevolent! This is why he has set up laws, like the law of sowing and reaping, the law of attraction, the law of seasons, etc. He wants us to discover and utilize these natural laws to produce all the abundance humans could ever need.

God is no fool. He would not have commanded us to populate the earth without making sure there was enough here to sustain the result of that command. I'm not suggesting that we shouldn't have a conservation ethic—we *do* need to replenish natural resources, like our forests. We need to keep our air and rivers clean, and so on. But there are vast resources on this planet that are yet to be utilized. One of God's Hebrew names is El Shaddai, which many theologians translate "the God who is more than enough." Maybe he really is more than enough.

We have to understand that when scarcity knocks at our door, there is always more out there. It may be hard to find at times, and it may take some ingenuity (and prayer) to figure out how to get it, but we must believe that there is always enough. Our faith in God as our Creator *demands* that we believe that. And experience has proven that to be the case.

More Than Enough

If we examine the earth's resources, we will come to a jarring conclusion: though the doomsayers continue to warn of resource shortages, the global economy is witnessing the greatest explosion of resource abundance in the history of humankind! If there really are physical limits to the sources of materials and energy that sustain the human population, then it appears that those limits are so far beyond the human horizon that they are for all intents and purposes *nonexistent.*

MIT professor Morris Adelman, one of America's foremost energy experts, said, "The great oil shortage is like the horizon, always receding as one moves toward it."[16] Consider that the world has nearly ten times the amount of proven oil reserves that it had in 1950 and almost twice the known reserves of 1970.

But here's what's interesting: two hundred years ago, petroleum was just a useless ooze that actually drove down property values. But somehow we humans discovered how to turn the ooze into a resource that improved and preserved life. The Scripture claims that it is God who promised to give human beings wisdom that would lead to "witty inventions"[17] and that through human history, "knowledge shall be increased."[18] Isn't it entirely possible that the God who commanded us to fill the earth knew when to strategically release knowledge and "witty inventions" to help sustain that command?

Sand has never been considered a resource, but the telecommunications revolution and our expanding technological capacity have turned sand into a valuable commodity—it's the basic resource from which computer chips and fiber-optic telecommunication devices are made.

What other undiscovered resources out there will improve and enrich life here on planet Earth? What else does God have up his sleeves to "show us his kindness" and "fill our hearts with joy"?[19]

Current nuclear technology ensures that the world has about 8,400 years of energy for the future at current rates of consumption.[20] If we continue to see advances in nuclear fusion technologies, it will guarantee vast supplies of energy for tens of thousands of years. If fusion proves to be a bust, there are geothermal and solar energy resources that promise virtually limitless supplies of energy as technology improves and those sources become more economically competitive.

Maybe the world really *isn't* a place of scarcity. What if there are enough surprises of provision from God's bounty to keep sustaining human life until the return of Christ? What if there is more than enough for everyone? That would make us want to fight things like poverty a little more tenaciously. That would make friends, businesses, communities, and nations a little less inclined to fight over resources.

Maybe the problem isn't scarcity but our reticence to trust—we would rather stockpile than trust. And maybe we have a reticence to trust because we don't want to have to think about finding the "more" that God promises is here—maybe it's a laziness issue. And since we don't want to *share* what we have, maybe it's also a greed issue.

Lots of maybes to consider.

Using the Law of Attraction to Secure Abundance

Believing that God is good enough to provide enough for every human being on the planet would make God a benevolent God indeed. But how do we tap into that abundance? Do we run after it and grovel for it? No. Jesus said, "Seek first the kingdom of God,"[21] which means we are to seek God's rule and his interests. We are also commanded to seek to understand how God set things up to work in this world.

There are mechanics to this—just as there are with the law of sowing and reaping. When the Bible discusses farming, it reminds us that God is the one responsible for the harvests and the fruit that the land brings forth.[22] Even so, no farmer sits around watching TV, expecting God to miraculously bring harvests of wheat and corn and barley, or *whatever*, to put in their silos. Farmers wait for the right season; they work the ground; they plant the seed; and they search for secrets to improve the farming enterprise. They learn about fertilizing, weed management, hybrid seed development—there's a whole science behind farming!

As farmers and agrarian scientists discover ways to make crops more bountiful, no one wonders if they have crossed the line into the domain of God. We believe that God is the one who gives humans wisdom to "work the system" *he* has put into place. And we believe he is worthy of praise after humans work the system and experience abundance. As seventeenth-century hymnist Thomas Ken sang, "Praise God from whom all blessings flow!"

Who Gets Blessed?

As I was tooling down the road in rural Wisconsin a number of years ago, a very large, well-kept farm caught my eye. Wisconsin is known for its family-owned farms—you usually pass one about every two miles on the roadways. This one was impressive indeed: beautiful yards, freshly painted white wood fences, striking farmhouse and outbuildings (the main barn even had a cute cow painted over the door), and the farm animals looked healthy and clean.

As I continued, the next farm I passed on the highway stood in stark contrast. It was completely disheveled. The yards looked as if goats mowed them. Wild wire "hairs" that resembled the eyebrows of a ninety-year-old man shot around each post of the wire fences. The porch on the house was leaning a tad to the south, and the barn door was unattached on one end—neither had seen a coat of paint in recent decades. And the farm animals were small and completely covered with clumps of cow dung.

Now, it doesn't take a lot of analysis to figure out what was going on. I'm sure one could argue that the farmer with the glorious farm was experiencing the blessing of God. And maybe the blessings wore out before it got down the road to the farmer with the farming disaster. But everyone knows there's more to that story. God blesses people, but he also blesses their *efforts*. The blessed farmer got off his "blessed assurance" and got to work. The not-so-blessed farmer didn't. And if they switched farms, it wouldn't be long before the look of the farms would switch as well.

Second-Cause Miracles

It's an easy matter for God to do special miracles of provision (remember Jesus feeding the five thousand with a few loaves of bread and a couple of pieces of fish?[23]). But it is no less a miracle of provision when we score harvests of blessings by learning to use the law of sowing and reaping, the law of attraction, and the law of "breaking into a sweat" as we go after the good that God has placed in this world.

Imagine if you had two boys, Bobby and Joey. And they came to you one morning, asking for money for new bikes that they wanted. You could just give them the money (a parental miracle?), but you are interested in teaching them how to be more than "takers" in the world. So you set up a system. Since you live by fields full of wildflowers, you tell them that you will give them one dollar for every bundle of wildflowers they pick.

Both boys hop right on it. But Bobby abandons Joey in the fields before noon. Joey is pouring with sweat and working as feverishly as he can. After a couple of hours Bobby arrives with eight of his friends—he's told them that he will give them each fifty cents for every bundle of wildflowers. By the end of the day, without breaking into much of a sweat, Bobby has all the money he needs for the new bike, but Joey only has about half—yet he's worked much harder.

Bobby is smiling, because he learned how to work the system that was set up. But Joey comes to you and tries to talk you into giving him *more* per bundle (he wants special treatment), arguing that he has worked much harder than Bobby. You have a decision to make.

I don't know about you, but I'd rather "work the system" that God set up than go back to God directly, asking him to do some special financial miracle for me. Asking for monetary miracles feels a little irresponsible to me—like a perfectly healthy, single, skilled worker living on food stamps. Don't misunderstand; I use divine "food stamps" with some degree of regularity—being a fallen person in a fallen world does not a perfect record make. But I think it brings God more glory when we trust and work the system of provision that he has set up (such as the law of attraction) than when we have to make a desperate 911-I-need-a-miracle-now, could-you-send-a-dog-with-a-bag-full-of-silver-dollars-in-his-mouth?" call to the Almighty.

But maybe that's just me.

8

A Dark "Secret"

The law of attraction, which is being heralded as "The Secret," becomes a "dark secret" when it is only tied to an individual's wants, lusts, and desires—not to anything "otherly," like the kingdom of God. When you live for yourself, the world becomes a place for "taking," a field of competition, a place for one-upping and conquering others—an environment where only the "fittest" survive. In this kind of world, polls matter, youth matters, beauty matters—the poor, weak, *un*beautiful, handicapped, aged, and anything less than a perfect "10" are all discarded and forgotten.

Being a Christ-follower challenges a life committed to self. Christianity begins with a poverty of spirit,[1] not with a false puffing up of one's own self-worth. Our goal is not to live big, grabbing all we can for ourselves. Our goal is to trust God to live big *in us* as we give ourselves for the good of others—especially those less fortunate than us.

Living for others causes us to participate in the Christ-pattern of surrender and obedience. This gets a little scary, because, in a way, it feels as though we lose our freedom as we follow a pathway of love. But it is only the self-oriented brand of freedom that is gradually and steadily lost as we love. And instead of feeling restricted by this kind of living, we actually discover (to our surprise and delight) whole new levels of freedom—a "selfless" brand! And it is *sweet*. This is the fulfillment of Jesus' claim that "he who loses his life . . . find[s] it."[2]

Certainly living for the kingdom of God is a kind of abandonment. It is a commitment to more than one's autonomous self. It is choosing to live a life that domesticates and decenters from the self, all the while trusting God to take over the center of the self. This is how a person steps into the freedom of loving God with the whole heart. But don't think this ends up being the destruction of our autonomy or self—it is not! It is the preservation and transformation of it, by taking it up into the dominion of God's kingdom. Here the believer meets God, learns to love, and experiences true fulfillment.

Hard for Hedonists

The concept of surrender and obedience, however, is totally foreign to most people in our culture. Ours is a society of hedonists. *Hedonism* is the belief that pleasure or happiness is the highest good. Hedonists are devoted to pleasure as a way of life. (Hmmm . . . dinner and a movie, anyone?) This is not to say that pleasure is evil; it is not. But making it your highest goal? Now we have a problem.

Our culture is not open to anything as horrifyingly *un*pleasurable as "surrender" or "obedience." We are way too self-indulgent. We believe the world is here for our own liberty, and we feel we should be allowed to get away with doing whatever it is we want, whenever we want to. Permissiveness and moral relativism are the only rules that matter in "Hedonville."

The idea of giving up one's will for the good of another is seen as ludicrous and a complete abdication of one's personal freedom. And you can't go there. No one messes with personal freedom—not in America. It's about the only value we hold sacrosanct in our culture. But hedonism has its problems. The truth is, this kind of radical, personal freedom ultimately results in a sense of aimlessness and inferiority. Alienation and anxiety are always the fruit of selfish freedom.

The Truth, and Nothing but the Truth

When you are devoted to pleasure, it is hard to face the truth about *anything*. You just want to hear what you want to hear, and anyone who tells you differently is perceived as the enemy—or at least as unloving. Don't misunderstand me; there is a time for the unqualified, uncritical support of others. When our kids were in kindergarten, they would bring home pieces of art. In all honesty they were disasters as far as art was concerned—six-year-olds do not make for good artists. But they were treasures to us! We'd gloat over them, praise our kids for them, and hang them conspicuously on the refrigerator door. The product was precious because our precious children made them. And the *un*critical support was critical to their developing self-esteem.

However, as our kids got older and more mature, we began to be more honest about what they were good at and what they were not so good at. Was that always easy? Of course not. But honesty is critical to responsible human development, and it keeps us out of the world of pure fantasy. When you hear honest feedback from those you love that you are not as good as you think you are, you have three choices:

1. Work harder to excel if you *really* want to do or be a certain thing. (Don't expect praise when your work is not praiseworthy.) Henry David Thoreau wrote, "If you have built castles in the air, your work need not be lost; that is where they should be. Now put the foundations under them." If you are not willing to work toward your dreams, not just "dream" them, then you are living in a fantasy world. And fantasy is not reality. *Get real.*

2. Ask for honest feedback from people you respect and if those "in the know" don't encourage you to continue moving down a particular path, reassess your strengths, and go a new direction. Receiving honest input may sound like cruel dream-smashing to you, but it's not—it's a *reality check.*

3. Blow off the assessments of those around you and dream your dream until reality and fantasy merge into one glorious vision—this is called growing and smoking your very own *dream-ganja.*

Whatever Happened to Work?

Another serious flaw in how the law of attraction is presented by the Byrne team is their silence about the need for serious, thoughtful, sweat-of-the-brow *work*. You get the feeling reading "the Secret" that all one has to do is think, feel good, and dream—that's it. Then everything comes to you magically; the universe does the rest. I believe that dreaming is powerful—thoughts and feelings are powerful. But there's more to the law of attraction than just sitting around and dreaming. You have to *do* stuff—boring, hard stuff, like persevering through school, or tenaciously saying no to buying more stuff or doing more fun things when you need to pay your bills first. And what of patience, determination, persistence, courage, fearlessness, steadfastness, and loyalty? These things can't be replaced by simply broadcasting *thoughts* and *feelings* out into the universe and expecting the cosmos to give you back everything you want—just because you're worth it. Whatever happened to the idea of *work*?

But who wants to work if the universe will do the work for you? Playing video games and watching *24* on TV is a lot more fun than taking some extra night courses at a local community college. Why work so hard and pay so much to enhance your career by going to school for a degree, when all you need to do is cut out pictures of new cars and million-dollar houses, imagine having them, and—*presto!*—wealth cometh. Think *and* grow rich is so much easier than think *plus* do, save, plan, curtail spending, engage in continuing education, and work yourself into a sweat and grow rich. But why do anything if the benevolent cosmos is simply awaiting your command?

Play on, dude.

The problem with sitting around and dreaming is it only works for the ones who write books and create DVDs *telling* everyone to sit around and dream. And when we buy those books, it proves to the authors that sitting around and dreaming really does work—at least for them. The rest of us have to work.

An *American Idol* Culture

The lines between fantasy and reality get constantly blurred in a culture committed to personal pleasure. To present the law of attraction to a culture like ours without acknowledging and warning against this seems philosophically irresponsible to me. A snapshot of our inability to separate fantasy from reality appears no more clearly than on the widely popular television series *American Idol*—a reality show that searches for vocal talent. The winner is given a shot at a career in performance singing.

In a recent season, a contestant from Minneapolis had his eyes on the prize of becoming the next "American idol," with all its glitz, glamour, and promised idol worship. After being rejected by the judges from advancing in the competition, he stormed out of the room. With angry tears streaming down his cheeks, he blurted one or two expletives at Simon Cowell and the other judges and exclaimed to the camera, "I'm already sixteen, and I wanted to start out successful."

He wanted to "start out" successful—not *work* toward it. (The hedonists' rule, I tell you!) He just couldn't understand why the judges would dare end what he had dreamed of doing. How could those #@!$@!% judges throw a roadblock in front of what he felt was his *right* to do?

Truth be told, there's a lot of you-owe-me-what-I-want-'cause-I'm-so-awesome-and-I-want-it people out there. There is a steady increase in people who feel they have the right to whatever they want in our culture. They aren't satisfied with the Declaration of Independence–bestowed right to the "pursuit of Happiness"; they think happiness is their right straight off—*no pursuit necessary*. Of course, happiness is not connected to anything so domestic and common as a good job, a simple life, and a happy marriage—no way. These boys and girls want it *all*. They want to be rich, famous, and appropriately worshipped and adored.

Sadly, being an "American Idol" culture is probably the main reason for the huge splash of success Rhonda Byrne has enjoyed with her recent best seller, *The Secret*—millions of copies have sold. Why? What nerve has it hit to trigger such an amazing response?

Thank you, hedonism. When the law of attraction is presented to a culture dedicated to personal pleasure and happiness; and that culture is told that "the Secret" is the key to getting *anything* you want, *anytime* you want it; and when the all-you-need-to-know-to-get-the-Secret-working-in-your-life information is seamlessly woven into a ninety-minute, no-brainer, slap-your-mamma DVD, with a cinematic flair rivaling *The Da Vinci Code*, you have yourself the makings of a hit. It's all just *so exciting* and *fun*. And you don't even have to do anything that requires discipline or that is as hard and boring as . . . let's say, reading.

What About Ethics?

Another *faux pas* for the Byrne team has to do with how they handle the issue of ethics. *Ethics* are the principles we live by—what we deem right and wrong as individuals and as a society. The currency at stake here is, *who gets to decide?* Hedonists will always assert that "what's right for you isn't necessarily right for me" and vice versa. They will fight for the notion that right and wrong are things that each person must decide for him- or herself—internally. To make such judgments is not the right of any *external* authority. Certainly not God.

Christian theology, on the other hand, holds that God is the author of ethics—as our Creator, he is the one who ultimately gets to make the call on what is right and what is wrong; which motives are good and which ones are bad. Scripture says that we can trust God in this because his judgments are ordered to something other than ego and pleasure—they are ordered to *his nature*, which is *love*.[3] This means that God never makes decisions arbitrarily—he doesn't insist "this is right" and "that is wrong" just because he is God and *can* mandate things. In other words, he isn't judging right from wrong because of some divine impulse to boss people around. His judgments are servants to his loving nature—he only demands what love demands. God is not selfish; he can be trusted.

God's dream in creating humans was for us to be in his image—to be like him.[4] God gave human beings the same power to choose that he enjoys. But what did he want us to do with it? Were we to start choosing things arbitrarily—deciding what is right or wrong on the basis of what we feel is right or wrong? Or was the human will to be "ordered to" something else—something higher than self-centered feelings or whims?

In one of the churches I pastored, there was a young boy who kept sneaking around and pulling the fire alarms in the church hallways. It took us several visits from the fire department before we caught the little fella. He believed that pulling fire alarms was something we do because we *can*. He didn't understand that fire alarms are to be "ordered to" a specific purpose—they should only be pulled to warn of a fire. The same holds true for our ability to choose. We should not choose because we *can*; our capacity to choose needs to be *ordered to* something else—God's love; there must be fire.

It was the great theologian Augustine (from way back in the fourth century) who first took the position that the fall of man was all about our "choosing" department—the human will. He held that God gave humans "will" so we could respond to God's right and wrong. Before the Fall in Genesis 3, Adam and Eve's right and wrong were *in God.* God told them what was right and what was wrong. They simply obeyed. Their wills were ordered to God's purposes.

Augustine claimed that this first sinful act *bent* (Lat., *incurvatus*) the human will. This made the human will do something it was never designed to do. It stopped ordering itself to (or obeying) God's right and wrong and started instead to determine right and wrong all on its own—ungoverned by God's loving character.

Augustine argued that the temptation of the serpent was to lure Adam and Eve into believing they shouldn't obey anyone but themselves—that right and wrong should be ascertained *within* themselves. Hence, their choice to eat the forbidden was really a decision to live a life of choosing right and wrong on their own—a decision to never again live in response to God and his nature of love. Obedience to God was no longer on the table; right and wrong became whatever humankind wanted it to be.

After the Fall, the will was no longer ordered to anything outside itself. It became a force unto itself. When human will was dislodged from a greater purpose, it was free to want whatever it wished. Selfishness was born. The problem of the human soul, then, is neither ignorance nor our desire for evil things; the problem is that we make up our own right and our own wrong. This is the worm that has curled its way into the apple of the human condition.

Ethical Vacuums

When human beings get used to making choices based on their own perception of right and wrong, we enter an ethical vacuum. There is no such thing as "right and wrong"—at least not a universal right and wrong. This is the dawning of moral relativism, which is the position that there are no moral or ethical absolutes or universal truths. Instead everything is *relative*. What's right or wrong needs to be determined by social, cultural, or personal circumstances. The preference of the individual rules supreme in a moral relativist's world—who cares about what anyone else thinks or values? These boys and girls argue that there is no one "right" way or one "wrong" way. So, "Do what you want—it's all good" is their credo. (FYI: This is also the intellectual fodder of the ethically deplorable third-world dictator.)

The truth is, your choices *do* impact more than yourself, and not recognizing that opens the floodgates for you to act in ways that hurt those around you. The sad thing is you won't feel the slightest tinge of guilt, because you won't even notice the pain you are inflicting—you are too focused on how things are affecting *you* to notice anyone else. Making your own needs, desires, and concerns job #1 in your life leaves you apathetic toward the needs and longings of others. You join the ranks of the ethically handicapped (and if you *believe* it hard enough, the universe will start giving you a special parking space).

Bruce Almighty

In the witty comedy *Bruce Almighty*, Bruce Nolan (played by Jim Carrey) is a television reporter in Buffalo, New York. At the end of a particularly horrifying day, Bruce angrily ridicules and rages against God about the poor job he is doing of being in control of everything. God (played by Morgan Freeman) responds by appearing to Bruce in human form and endowing him with divine powers. He then challenges Bruce to see if he can do God's job any better.

At first Bruce uses his newfound powers for himself. In the name of sweet romance, he lassoes the moon and brings it extremely close to the planet—for no other reason than to get his girlfriend "in the mood" for love. Bruce is oblivious to the fact that his action is going to wreak havoc on the ocean tides. And he shows no hesitation in the least as he changes the orbit of the moon to enhance his romantic goal. After all, how could any action based on the pursuit of something as wonderful as love—something that feels so good—ever be wrong? The next morning, Bruce completely ignores the news reports of the disaster taking place on the coastlines, where tidal waves are destroying homes and lives as a result of the moon leaving its orbit the night before.

The Secret becomes a *dark secret* when it creates a culture of Bruce Almightys who use it solely to get whatever they want to get, without so much as a hint that what they "want" may be hurtful to, or even displace, someone else around them.

If you don't realize that there is more to the law of attraction than getting what you want, whenever you want it, you will be reduced to living in a world of fantasy and manipulation—the concept becomes dark indeed.

Fantasy and Manipulation 101

You understand that the law of attraction will bring you *anything* you want. And one of the things you want is a new couch. You have wanted one for a while. So you begin to work the law—you start thinking about it; you feel the feelings of having the new couch; you pore over magazines to find the one that is just right for you; and then you find it in a Dwell catalog (ahh . . . your first evidence that the law of attraction is working)—so you cut out the picture and put it on your refrigerator. Now you're convinced that the law of attraction is pulling it toward you *right now!*

You then discover that the more you think about the couch, *the more you want it.* Desire is in full bloom—you can hardly get it out of your mind. You're not concerned that it's lust or anything; you tell yourself it's just the law of attraction kicking in, perhaps with a vengeance. Then, magically, a new credit card shows up in the mail, with a limit just high enough to cover the designer couch! You know your family is pretty strapped financially, but that seems to be a smaller matter to the "miracle" you just witnessed. You are certain that the law of attraction has responded to your thoughts, feelings, and visualizations and has brought you that credit card! Now you can buy the couch! You would like to tell your husband, but you're not sure he's ready for the Secret yet—he's not really all that open to such things.

Sure, it will be tight adding another high-interest credit-card payment to your list of bills, but the law of attraction has gotten you the new couch—it will surely bring you some money to pay for it later (maybe the universe will bring your husband a *third* job!). Besides, you want it; that's all that's really important. Who cares if your husband already feels stretched and overloaded with dread as he slaves to make ends meet. *You want this.* And your thoughts of attraction are surely granting it. Feel the freedom! Giggle a little. Go ahead and marshal whatever you can to get what you want. Your wants are sovereign, and, by golly, you deserve it!

Right?

Fantasy and Manipulation 201

You have your eye on that new car. You don't know exactly how you are going to afford it, but you have it in your thoughts, and the law of attraction is revving its engine. With passion that makes you cross your fingers, you are trusting that the frequency for your new car is going out loud and clear. *It's-a-comin',* you keep telling yourself—you've asked, you've believed, and it's "receiving" time. You pretend you're driving it as you maneuver the old clunker you are stuck with; you tape a picture of your dream machine on the dashboard—*and* on your bathroom mirror; you imagine the feelings, the smells, the joy you will feel when you actually have it. You're tingling now.

Then a thought hits you out of the blue: *Maybe I could sell the car I have to one of my friends for more than it's really worth—I could talk it up, get them all excited, and then they would give me enough for a down payment for a lease on my new car.*

What a miraculous idea! The universe has sent it to you. How could it be ethically wrong? You're going to get what *YOU* want. If someone is getting hurt, that's just because he doesn't know *The Secret* yet—and that's his own fault. It's only $29.99 at Amazon.com.

Keeping It Safe

Whether we care to admit it or not, when hedonists use this particular make of the law of attraction, it becomes a devious recipe for material greed, social apathy, and victim blaming. The only way we can be certain that we are not just using it as a cover-up for selfishness and greed is to remain suspicious of ourselves. We have to remember that we humans have a penchant for self-deception. Our human pride does not like to accept our wretchedness—or our need for a Savior. We believe that we are to always do our best to keep feeling good about ourselves. The mortal sin of a hedonistic culture is negative self-esteem.

But what if we are not supposed to feel good about ourselves? What if we really *are* bad? A fallen people? Perhaps it is as the comic-strip character Pogo so aptly put it, "We have met the enemy, and it is us." Then our problem would not be one of negative self-esteem; we would simply have negative *selves*.

If we grasp this, we understand the need for a continual cultivation of desperation for God. Paul Tournier wrote, "Those who are the most pessimistic about man are the most optimistic about God."[5]

It is only when we stay tethered to God that the so-called Secret isn't a dark one.

9

A Tale of Two Stories

Imagine that you happened across a man one day, giving a speech in the open air in 1863. If you were a Martian, you would probably place little significance on what was going on. You'd most likely assume that humans occasionally like to stand on big boxes and make sounds. If you were a child on the scene, you would hope the speech would be brief—after all, adults' words, to you, are little more than a Charlie Brownesque *mwa, mwa, mwa, mwa, mwa*. You wouldn't have gotten much out of it. But, let's say you were a historian visiting from the future. Watching this speech by Abraham Lincoln at Gettysburg, Pennsylvania, would have definitely carried special meaning for you.

My point is that your *point of view*—where you are "coming from"—impacts how you interpret events, what you make of life, and ultimately how you respond to it. Your "take" on what is *really* going on around you—what you believe the story is—in due course shapes your life. It will also impact how you approach and try to utilize the law of attraction.

So, what in the world *is* going on? Is God controlling things? Are

103

human beings masters of their own fate? Are God and humans coworkers together? If so, how does that "cooperation" work? Or do things just happen on their own? What's *your* take? What do you think is the backstory behind the events you see going on in the world?

A Lord of the Rings Culture

J. R. R. Tolkien's middle-earth saga, *Lord of the Rings*, depicted a fantasy world filled with all kinds of beings: from the familiar Humans, Hobbits, Elvens, Dwarvens, Dragons, Orcs, and Trolls, to the less-known Barlogs, Nazguls, Ents, and Woses. All of these races had differing histories, beliefs, credos, cultures, ethical codes, and legends—how they interpreted *reality* was different; their stories were diverse. And the stories they believed shaped the lives they lived. Philosophically, the West is as divergent in its beliefs and interpretations of daily events as the creatures from Tolkien's middle-earth.

The apostle Paul warned about this. He said that, in a world of contrasting stories and interpretations, those holding differing points of view will always try to *squeeze* us into agreeing with them. Each alternate story claimed certain things about God (or the gods), the role of the human race (who we are), and what the future holds. Paul challenged the church not to be "conformed" by the stories concocted by people.[1] The Scriptures, he said, tell us the story from God's point of view, and if we will listen to and embrace that story, our lives will be "transformed."[2]

Let's look at two prevailing stories (metanarratives) that dominate Western culture. One is of faith in God, the other of faith in humankind.

The Short Version

At the risk of sounding overly simplistic, here is a short version of the biblical story: Reality as we know it is the result of a God who created everything we see. Yet, he is not limited by what he made—he lives both *inside* (immanent) and *outside* (transcendent) of creation. He created the world because he wanted to be a part of it—to flood his life *into* it. As part of a means to this end, he created a race of beings that would be able to represent his wisdom and care within creation. And he made them to be a little different from everything else in creation, to be bearers of something unique—he "breathed" into us (not into any other creature) his very breath.[3] His breath in the human life was the chief way God was entering his creation. He wanted his glory to be present in this world *through* the human experience.

But in tragic irony the very beings God created for him to have access into the world rebelled against his intention; we lost our way. We also lost access to his breath—his *presence*. We died spiritually, and creation was alienated from its Creator.[4] The good news is that not only is God a Creator, but he is also a Redeemer and a Restorer. God found a completely appropriate way to resolve the problem by finding a way to reconnect with the human race and bring his original intention to pass. Jesus Christ came to this planet (entered the limitations of creation) to take on *our* spiritual death, and he found a way to re-"breath" us—to cause us to be, in a spiritual sense, born all over again.[5] Through Jesus coming into our lives, God once again indwells his human creatures,[6] as he will ultimately do with all of creation (the end of the Bible says that God will come to live on planet Earth someday!), transforming it into what it was made for from the beginning.[7]

Wow. Great story.

Appropriate Management

I don't think that believing in God and his plan for our lives means we are reduced to being puppets. Nor do I think that God is interested in mandating who we're to marry, exactly what job we're each supposed to have, and just what we're to eat for dinner. He doesn't want to micromanage our lives.

I think God is more like a parent. Gail and I have four children (all adults now). We certainly had a "will" for them: We wanted them to be happy. We wanted them to grow up to be responsible, contributing individuals. We urged them to dig for and discover their talents and interests, and then invest them. We wanted them each to find someone to love and enjoy. We had a whole bunch of specific things we willed for them—specific and yet general enough to *not* be controlling or repressive. We did not want to run their lives.

I think this mirrors how God approaches his will for us. He has a specific will for each of us. He wants us: to be happy;[8] to live moral and ethical lives;[9] to process our failure with forgiveness,[10] thus remaining free from any sense of condemnation;[11] to live long, satisfying lives;[12] to be fruitful in our endeavors;[13] to impact the world;[14] to be free from addictions and destructive behavior patterns;[15] to feel complete;[16] and so on.

These are all very specific things that he wills for us—specific and yet general enough to *not* be oppressive. He does not want to run our lives.

The Goldilocks Principle

It's kind of strange when you think about it, but as believers, we're living our whole lives loving and serving someone we've never seen. But that's the way faith works. God is invisible. Yet we see hints of his activity all around us. Mathematical genius Blaise Pascal, who lived in the 1600s, wrote, "If [God] had wished to overcome the obstinacy of the most hardened, he could have done so by revealing himself to them so plainly that they could not doubt the truth of his essence. . . . There is enough light for those who desire only to see, and enough darkness for those of a contrary disposition."[17]

I think God sneaks around in our lives in the same way as did Goldilocks in "Goldilocks and the Three Bears." Let me explain. In the Goldilocks story, Mama, Papa, and Baby Bear come home one day, only to discover that *someone* had been eating their porridge, sitting in their chairs, and lying on their beds. It isn't till the end of the story that they find out it was *Goldilocks.*

I believe God, in Goldilocks fashion, gets involved with our lives *before* we notice him. He messes with our porridge (touches our souls in a way that makes certain things more interesting to us than others); sits in our chairs (he's the one who enables us to cry over the things we cry over and laugh about what is funny to us); he lies on our beds (he fashions us in such a way that we find some things fulfilling and others not; there are places that feel "right" to us and others that don't). And though he is the one who does it, and we see and feel the *results,* we don't get to see *him* till the end of the story. The old song goes, "When we all get to heaven, what a day of rejoicing that will be."[18]

Free to Be

Don't fear that submitting to God's will means there is only *one specific thing* that you are allowed to do—marry a specific person or hold a specific career—or else God will be angry with you. That is not true. As long as the directionality of your heart is to love God and you are open to his influence in your life, you have the freedom to run at the things that bring you joy, love, happiness, and laughter. *Go for it!* God intended for life to be an adventure. He wants us to enjoy it.

Discover the things that give you inner happiness—those are the things that will fuel your success. Find what makes you feel good, what resonates with your heart, and you will find yourself right in the center of God's will. Unless God makes it clear that he wants something else for you (he will sometimes ask you to participate in special projects), you can live in the joy that you are completely in his will.

Plans with Caveats

Though we should have a great sense of freedom when it comes to personal choice, the apostle James admonished folks to always keep an attitude of submission before God as they made their plans. Why? Simply because "the LORD is God. It is he who made us, and we are his; we are his people, the sheep of his pasture."[19]

James warns, "And now I have a word for you who brashly announce, 'Today—at the latest, tomorrow—we're off to such and such a city for the year. We're going to start a business and make a lot of money.'" But his "word" of warning has nothing to do with the actual planning process. He simply tells them to add this caveat: "Instead, make it a habit to say, 'If the Master wills it and we're still alive, we'll do this or that.'"[20]

We don't have to be nervous about planning our lives—we can think and dream and put the law of attraction in motion for any future we would like. It is fine to do that. But we must always give God right of veto! Why would God ever veto? Because he knows the future and will sometimes warn us if we are making a bad choice. That's a good thing.

Solomon echoed this when he penned, "Trust God from the bottom of your heart; don't try to figure out everything on your own. Listen for God's voice in everything you do, everywhere you go; he's the one who will keep you on track."[21] Notice there is no challenge issued about making sure you *only* do what (or go where) God *specifically* tells you. That's just not the case. Take your liberty, but as you go, listen for God's voice. It's OK to make choices about life. Just make sure you acknowledge God in the process and obey him if he says no or seems to be leading you another direction.

God Is Not Grandpa

Life should be enjoyable. God designed it to be that way. But there are times when God makes life uncomfortable for us. If we trust him, it's no big deal. If we don't, it can escalate into trouble in the blink of an eye.

Just as God tells us to discipline our children, he disciplines us too because he loves us. And if we do not discipline them, we, in effect, *hate* them.[22] Don't think that God's *only* concern is for us to be content. Don't confuse God with Grandpa. Grandpa tends to overlook wrongdoing, and he always avoids confrontation. Grandpa's only goal at the end of the day is that all had a good time. But Jesus didn't tell us to pray, "Our Grandpa in heaven." He said to pray, "Our Father in heaven."[23]

Scripture is clear. God is our Father, and he "disciplines us for our good, that we may share in his holiness."[24] God doesn't just love us with a smile as he distributes playful impulses of joy into our souls. When we are living selfishly, unethically, or sinfully, he gets hard with us and treats us in a way that doesn't seem "pleasant at the time, but painful."[25] He does so because we are his sons and daughters. We are the chosen, his sent ones. He believes in us, trusts us, and calls upon us to represent him. You and I matter. The Bible applauds one guy who "served God's purpose in his own generation."[26] That's what he wants all of us to do. That's why we are here.

If we say no to his plan, he will back off. That is a scary enterprise. When Israel said no to God, he said of them, "My people would not listen to me; Israel would not submit to me. So I gave them over to their stubborn hearts to follow their own devices."[27]

I don't want to be left to my "own devices," do *you*?

The Prophets Are Coming

Because of his commitment to us as Father, there are many times you will hear God speaking to you in ways that make you feel uncomfortable. God told his people in Israel, "Day after day, again and again I sent you my servants, the prophets."[28]

God always sends "the prophets." Sometimes the prophets are pastors and friends who remind us to give more thought to prayer and our spiritual lives. Other times they are programs and organizations who urge us to attend to social justice issues in the community, drawing our attention to those issues and people being neglected by our government. The prophets are usually the ones paying for the advertising, telling us of the dangers of smoking or driving under the influence. The prophets are parents encouraging their children to act responsibly in the world. They are also the ones confronting us with the fact that saving money is not a good enough reason to make an illegal copy of music or computer software or to cheat on our taxes.

The prophets are everywhere. And as uncomfortable as it is, we need to listen to them.

An Alternative Story

The other prevailing story vying for belief in our culture is very different from the Bible story. In this story there is no Creator-God, no prophets, no judgment, and certainly no "divine plan" to concern yourself with.

The universe is the product of random chance—a roll of the dice. In this story, things that exist must have always been here; there was no creation event. Matter exists, and that is *all* that matters. Astrophysicist Carl Sagan (in mocking liturgical tone), narrates the story well: "The Cosmos is all there is, or ever was, or ever will be."[29]

For this crowd, the universe is simply a closed system—like the plumbing in a house. It is not open to being *reordered* from the outside by any transcendent Being such as God. There are no miracles. If there is a god, he or she is irrelevant. History has no reason, no overarching purpose; it is just what happens—a sequential, linear stream of cause-and-effect events.

Who we are, in this view, is really no one in particular. We are not special or chosen. We arrived here because our number came up, like a number in a Las Vegas game. There is no such thing as destiny. No one is looking out for us or planning anything for us. Human beings are just complex machines that have personality because of chemical and physical interactions that we do not fully understand. The mystery of life is not genuine mystery; it is mechanical complexity.

Death, from this standpoint, is not a transition from one kind of living to another; it is simply the extinction of personality and individuality. According to the popular twentieth-century philosopher Ernest Nagel, "Human destiny [is] an episode between two oblivions."[30] Pretty dark.

Believing that the universe is here by chance gives particular shape to one's responses in life. Ethics, for example (our moral sense of right and wrong), ends up being a purely human thing. If one accepts this story, the stage is set for the apostles of absurdity to convince *anyone* of *anything*—for all ideas and creeds would be equally valid.

Mr. Universe

In a reality without a Creator, the universe is seen as a giant clock, whose gears and levers mesh with mechanical precision, ticking and tocking through time in a perfectly ordered way—all on its own, of course. God is not immanent, not fully personal, and certainly not providential (there is no divine plan).

If you buy into this story wholesale, there's a fairly good chance that the shape or order of your life would be characterized by a kind of me-first, I'm-going-to-grab-all-the-marbles-I-can gusto—after all, there is no God looking out for you. You need to fend for yourself.

Again, there are no miracles in this story. Humans aren't fallen. We are just part of the mechanics, and it is up to us to stay in sync with the rest of the gears and levers (including books like *The Secret*). There is no sin or shame, no grace or accompanying presence of God, and no Judgment Day—party on! Each human needs to learn to make the best of things—to go with the flow and not get caught in the gears of life.

When people who believe this rendition use the concepts in *The Secret,* you hear statements like the following:

- The Universe at large is like a genie (and *universe* is most often spelled with a capital *U*, which gives one that the-universe-needs-to-replace-my-concept-of-God kind of feeling).

- The Universe awaits you to tell it what to do. It says to you, "Your wish is my command."

- The Universe is your holy guardian angel, your higher self.

- Make a command to the Universe; let it know what you want.

- The Universe responds to your thoughts.

- Humans are learning to use more and more of the mind; one day we will be able to go anywhere, do anything, achieve all—there will be no limit to what we will be able to do.

- The Universe is your catalog. Just flip through it and say, "I'd like to have that product, this experience, that person." It's *that* easy . . .

- The Universe will rearrange itself to make things happen for you.

- You can have whatever you choose; the Universe doesn't care how big it is. There is no judgment, no right or wrong.

- The Universe will deliver every single thing that you've been wanting.

Wow. This is a very different concept from the one God teaches.

Buying into these lies orders and shapes your life in significant ways. These beliefs force one to view the universe as mechanical: purposeless and cold. There would be no such thing as prayer, except for a kind sounding much like the verses of an old Steven Crane poem from the 1800s:

A man said to the universe:

> "Sir, I exist."
> "However," replied the universe,
> "The fact has not created in me
> a sense of obligation."[31]

115

The Story Matters

Which set of beliefs you hold to be true will profoundly impact the way you feel about yourself and how you respond to the things that happen to you. If this is really a dice-tossed world, then life is just a race of the rats, and it's every rat for him- or herself. If the Bible is true, it is a pretty wild story—and it's one that means we matter. It also means that what you and I do and how we live matters, because we are being defined from an eternal place—we are part of something bigger than ourselves, part of a story that God is telling. This is a story in which we are the predestined, and our primary job is to make space for God to inhabit the world.

Methinks it's a better story.

10

The Real "Secret"

When I first viewed Rhonda Byrne's DVD rendition of *The Secret*, I felt ambivalent—grieved, then encouraged; encouraged, then grieved. Grieved because of the absence of any meaningful connection with God or the claims of Christ; encouraged because the longing for a better life is evidence that people are reaching out beyond themselves. And I believe if they continue to reach out, they will eventually run into God and the claims of Christ.

There is a very provocative story in the life of the apostle Paul where he evidences the kind of ambivalence I'm referring to here. It was when he visited the pagan city of Athens on one of his missionary journeys. Christ had never been preached in Athens, and Paul was amazed at how religious the city was. It was full of idols and idol worship.

At first, the Bible says, Paul was "greatly distressed"[1]—grieved, as it were. But as he continued to walk around, he found something that encouraged him about the Athenian situation—there was evidence that God's kingdom was at work in their midst. The proof of that,

Paul claimed, was the fact that they were "very religious."[2] He pointed to an altar, which had been built to an unknown God and declared, "I'm here to introduce you to this God so you can worship intelligently, know who you're dealing with."[3]

He then told the Athenians that God had always been with them; that he had even "determined the times set for them and the exact places where they should live."[4] (Think of that. God destined them to be in Athens—though it was not a Christian city.) And Paul claims that God did this so people "would seek him" and "find him" because he was "not far from each one of [them]."[5] He even maintained that *all* people are wrapped in God's care—that "in him we live and move and have our being."[6]

This story is stunning to me. Paul was saying that God was present and working in that pagan culture *before* Paul got there with the gospel of Jesus Christ! God was responsible for their impulse to worship. But he clarifies that this "working" was incomplete and unclear without the addition of the gospel. The *gospel,* or "good news," was needed to unpack God's dream for humanity and to give instruction as to the why and directionality of worship. But, Paul's point is clear—whether people see what is going on or not, God still works in the life of *every* person, in *every* nation, at *every* moment. Most just don't know it, and they build "altars" to what they don't understand.

That is my take on the popularity of *The Secret.* People are rushing to this information because they are looking for hope, longing for change, and seeking a new way of living that is not limited or oppressive. But without realizing it, people are really looking for Jesus and the "new creation" he brings.[7]

There's No Water Here

Scripture claims that God has "set eternity in the hearts of men."[8] Awkwardly stated, God has put a "God-hole" in the hearts of people that can only be filled with God. To try to fill that hole with anything else (dreams, goals, goods, accomplishments, applause, beauty, success) will leave one still feeling empty in the end (just ask the Britney Spearses of the world).

The psalmist wrote, "O God, you are my God; I earnestly search for you. My soul thirsts for you; my whole body longs for you in this parched and weary land where there is no water."[9] There is *nothing* on this planet that will quench the God-thirst of the human soul. Referring to the God-thirsty masses, Henry David Thoreau wrote, "The mass of men lead lives of quiet desperation."[10] The only cure for this thirst is found in the person of Jesus Christ—not in utilizing the law of attraction to realize health, wealth, and success on this planet.

Jesus tells the woman at the well, "If you knew the gift of God and who it is that asks you for a drink, you would have asked him and he would have given you living water."[11] Then he tells her, "Everyone who drinks the water of this well will be thirsty again, but whoever drinks the water I give him will never thirst. Indeed, the water I give him will become in him a spring of water welling up to eternal life."[12]

People are thirsty. The recent swell of interest in *The Secret* and other books like it is more evidence of that. But drinking water found only on the earth will still leave people "thirsty again." Jesus is the only "thirst quencher."

We're in Trouble

Here's some bad news: Humans are fallen. We are bankrupt. We need help outside of ourselves. Ever since the tragic Fall in Genesis 3, every person born is a kind of "born loser." The apostle Paul wrote, concerning the human race, "No one is righteous—not even one,"[13] and all have "sinned" and "fall short" of what God intended.[14] Each of us is deeply flawed because of sin. C.S. Lewis wrote of the nature of man, "Look for yourself and you will find in the long run only hatred, loneliness, despair, rage, ruin and decay."[15] Not a pretty picture.

The good news is, God looks past all the bad in us and places value on us. Scripture claims that he did this "while we were still sinners."[16] Sadly, modern psychology repudiates the whole concept that people are bad, because its supporters have witnessed how debilitating and destructive unresolved guilt is to our lives. In an attempt to reduce feelings of guilt, they tell people that there is no such thing as right and wrong—no such thing as *sin*. Right and wrong can only be determined on an individual basis. They urge folks to feel only "warm fuzzies" about themselves, to center on their good traits and learn to embrace and even welcome the bad about themselves. They tout artless platitudes like, "I'm OK, you're OK," in an attempt to trivialize the intensity of guilt that people feel.

But what modern psychology fails to recognize is that guilt, like physical pain, is actually a gift from God! Can you imagine if you could not feel pain? You'd lean over on a kitchen knife and be oblivious to a cut that could ultimately lead to your bleeding to death. Pain protects us and guards us in life. The capacity for guilt was given to us for the same reason.

Paul tells us that God's law was given so "everyone in the world may realize his guilt before God."[17] The realization of guilt becomes a kind of "schoolteacher" for us, leading us to Christ.[18] God never intended for guilt to go unresolved. Its resolve is found in the blood of Jesus. He meant for guilt to motivate us to come to him—not to be an end in itself.

The Secret Behind the "Secret"

Though we are to do what we can to help others hear about Jesus, the Scripture is clear that Satan tries to blind folks from understanding of the gospel. Paul writes, "The Good News we preach *is hidden* behind a veil . . . Satan, who is the god of this world, has *blinded the minds* of those who don't believe. They are unable to see the glorious light of the Good News. They don't understand this message about the glory of Christ."[19]

The New Testament also claims that there is a great *secret* tucked into the gospel of Christ: "This message was kept *secret* for centuries and generations past, but now it has been revealed to God's people. For God wanted them to know that the riches and glory of Christ are for you Gentiles, too. And *this is the secret*: Christ lives in you. This gives you assurance."[20]

It turns out that the *secret* behind the Secret is Christ himself—not just the law of attraction. This is what Satan tries to blind people from understanding. Apart from Jesus Christ, there really is no lasting peace—he is the Prince of Peace.[21] Apart from Christ, there really is no victory over sin and heartache—he is our victory.[22] Apart from Jesus Christ there is no completeness,[23] no real life—"he who has the son has life."[24]

As believers, we should use the law of attraction (and any other law that will help us be more effective in life), but we must shift the basis for happiness away from *laws*—our happiness needs to remain firmly rooted in a *Person*, Jesus Christ and our trust in him. Once, while recounting Israel's sins to the prophet Jeremiah, God said, "My people have done two sinful things: They have turned away from me, the well of living waters. And they have cut out of the rock wells for water for themselves. [But] they are broken wells that cannot hold water."[25]

People still do this today. They forget (or don't know) that Jesus is the only thirst quencher—the "well of living waters"—and they try to dig "wells" for themselves to quench their own thirst: perhaps a quest for success, a run at fame, a lust for money. Or they journey into darker things, like drug and alcohol abuse or illicit sexual behavior—these are all "wells that cannot hold water."

Years ago an old friend of my wife Gail's and mine, Nancy Arndt, wrote a piece that captures the God-thirst present in every person and how we run at other things to try to fill it:

> *He is the Security you seek in money*
> *He is the High you seek in alcohol*
> *He is the Ecstasy you seek in sex*
> *He is the Health you seek in doctors*
> *He is the Song you seek in music*
> *He is the Dance you seek in the clubs*
> *He is the Beauty you seek in travel*
> *He is the Wisdom you seek in books*
> *He is the Peace you seek in worry*
> *It is Jesus whom you seek . . .*[26]

The bottom line to all this is, *there's more to the Secret*—it's Jesus.

If you have never received him before, *stop, drop,* and *roll* . . . call out to him, and he will meet you where you are. Do it today. Here's a simple prayer to help you do just that:

Jesus, something in me is nudging me to say YES to you. I want to do that. The Bible says that if I declare you as the one in charge of my life—as Lord of my life—then help from heaven will come—that I will be "saved."[27] *I'm so open to that. Jesus, be my Lord—right here, right now, over my current set of circumstances—be my Lord. Forgive me of my sin. Cleanse me from the pursuits that I know are wrong. I surrender to you and welcome you into my life. I am yours!*

If you prayed this prayer from your heart, welcome to the journey of faith! Decide to press in and become a fully devoted follower of Jesus. Buy a Bible and start reading (even if you don't understand a lot of it). Find a church jammed with people who love Jesus and like to talk about the Bible (but steer clear from mean Bible people—they're pretty easy to spot: they think they are the only right ones, so they yell a lot and don't smile much). If you continue to cultivate a "yes" in your heart towards God—he will lead you![28]

Also, stay tenacious in your faith. Don't give up. There will be some hard times ahead—the negative forces in our world will not idly stand by and watch you become great for God. They will fight you the whole way! Jesus said, "In this world you will have trouble." But then he went on to say, "But be brave! I have defeated the world!"[29]

If this is the first time you have prayed this prayer, shoot me an e-mail: mailto:ed@edgungor.com. Heaven throws parties over this stuff.[30] I want to give out a shout as well.

Notes

1 Gods and Genies

1. 1 Corinthians 3:21–22.
2. Galations 6:7.
3. Luke 6:36–38 NASB.
4. Acts 17:26.
5. Psalms 139:16.
6. Psalms 100:3.
7. Genesis 45:18.
8. Matthew 10:39.
9. Arnold Toynbee, quoted in Joseph Tetlow, "The Human Person and Sexuality," *The Way Supplement,* 71 (1991), 44.
10. James 4:14.
11. James 4:15.
12. Mark 9:23.

2 Thoughts Become Things

1. Proverbs 23:7, author's paraphrase.
2. Rhonda Byrne, *The Secret* (TS Production, LLC, 2006), DVD.
3. Ibid.
4. 2 Corinthians 4:4 NLT.
5. See Ephesians 6:11–12, Acts 10:38, Luke 13:16, and John 13:27.
6. 2 Peter 1:4.

7. 2 Corinthians 10:4–5 NLV, emphasis added.

8. Philippians 4:8 MSG.

9. Job 3:25.

10. Byrne, *The Secret*, x–xi.

11. Genesis 1:31.

12. N. T. Wright, *Evil and the Justice of God* (Downers Grove, IL: IVP Books, 2006), 38–39.

13. See Revelation 21.

14. Matthew 5:46 MSG.

15. Acts 14:16 MSG.

16. Acts 17:25 NLT.

17. Mark 9:23.

18. Mark 11:24.

3 Using the Law of Attraction

1. Byrne, *The Secret*, 25.

2. Revelation 5:8.

3. 2 Corinthians 2:15–16.

4. Klaus Koch, *The Prophets: The Babylonian and Persian Periods* (Philadelphia: Fortress Press, 1989), 20.

5. Jeremiah 4:18 MSG.

6. Lisa Nicols, quoted in *The Secret*, 31–32.

7. Marci Shimoff, quoted in *The Secret*, 32.

8. Jack Canfield, quoted in *The Secret*, 178, emphasis added.

9. Neale Donald Walsch, quoted in *The Secret*.

10. W. Beron Wolfe, quoted in Lillian Eichler Watson, ed., *Light from Many Lamps* (New York: Simon and Schuster, 1951), 84.

11. Bill Hybels, *Who You Are When No One's Looking: Choosing Consistency, Resisting Compromise* (Downers Grove, IL: Intervarsity Press, 1987), 70–71.

12. Byrne, *The Secret*, 31.

13. Ibid., 33.
14. Deuteronomy 8:17–18 MSG.

4 I've Got a Feeling

1. Luke 12:16–21 MSG.
2. See Romans 8:2.
3. 1 John 5:19.
4. Byrne, *The Secret*, 37.
5. Ephesians 2:1–3 NLV.
6. Colossians 1:13 MSG.
7. Bob Proctor, quoted in *The Secret*, 37.
8. 2 Corinthians 10:4 NKJV.
9. Matthew 11:28–30 MSG.
10. Jeremiah 29:11 MSG.
11. 2 Corinthians 10:4.
12. Peter Scazzero, *Emotionally Healthy Spirituality, Unleash a Revolution in Your Life in Christ* (Franklin, TN: Integrity Publishers, 2006), 24.
13. Ibid., 26.
14. Ibid., 53, adapted.
15. See Romans 5:8.
16. Hebrews 5:14 NASB.
17. Adapted from Paul Brand and Phillip Yancey, *Pain: The Gift Nobody Wants* (Darby, PA: Diane Publishing Co., 1999), 6–7.

5 Why Christians Get Nervous About This

1. *The Food Defect Action Levels* (College Park, MD: U.S. Food and Drug Administration, May 1995, rev. May, 1998), http://vm.cfsan.fda.gov/~dms/dalbook.html.
2. See Matthew 23:22.
3. Proverbs 23:7, author's paraphrase.

6 How Christians Should Use the Law of Attraction

1. Matthew 4:8–9 NKJV.
2. See Matthew 10:38–39.
3. Ecclessiastes 2:10–11.
4. Hebrews 11:13.
5. Hebrews 11:16.
6. Psalms 17:14.
7. 1 John 2:15–17 MSG.
8. Hebrews 11:24–27 MSG.
9. Matthew 20:28.
10. Philippians 4:19.
11. Pope John Paul II, quoted in *Living God's Justice: Reflections and Prayers* (Cincinnati: St. Anthony Messenger Press, 2006), 11.
12. Genesis 11:6 AMP.
13. Genesis 30:37.
14. Genesis 30:39.
15. Acts 2:17.
16. Isaiah 43:18–19.
17. Habakkuk 2:14.
18. Matthew 5:13–14.
19. Mark 11:24.
20. *The Book of Common Prayer* (New York: Oxford University Press, 1990), 258.
21. Acts 2:17.
22. Psalms 2:8.
23. Ephesians 3:20, emphasis added.
24. Revelation 21:3–4.
25. Mark 1:15 KJV.
26. Matthew 6:10 KJV, emphasis added.

27. Hebrews 6:5.
28. *The Book of Common Prayer*, 138.
29. Hebrews 6:12.

7 The Law of Attraction and Money

1. Acts 20:35.
2. Genesis 14:23.
3. 1 Kings 3:11–13.
4. Matthew 6:29.
5. See Luke 8:2–3.
6. See John 13:29.
7. Ephesians 4:28.
8. Ibid.
9. Genesis 2:12.
10. Revelation 21:21.
11. Genesis 1:31.
12. Genesis 1:28.
13. Exodus 16:20.
14. Matthew 6:31.
15. Matthew 6:34.
16. Morris Adelman, "Oil Fallacies," *Foreign Policy* 82 (Spring 1991), 10.
17. Proverbs 8:12 KJV.
18. Daniel 12:4 KJV.
19. See Acts 14:17.
20. William Nordhaus, "Resources as a Constraint on Growth?" *American Economic Review* 64, no. 2 (May 1974), 25.
21. Matthew 6:33 NKJV.
22. See Acts 14:17.
23. Mark 6:39–44.

8 A Dark "Secret"

1. See Matthew 5:3.
2. Matthew 10:39 NKJV.
3. See Psalms 19:9; 119:39, 75, 137, 156.
4. Genesis 1:26.
5. Paul Tournier, *Guilt and Grace* (New York: Harper and Row, 1959), 159.

9 A Tale of Two Stories

1. Romans 12:2 NKJV.
2. Ibid.
3. Genesis 2:7.
4. Romans 8:20–21.
5. See John 3:3.
6. Colossians 1:27.
7. See Revelation 21–22.
8. Nehemiah 8:10.
9. 1 Peter 1:15.
10. 1 John 1:9.
11. Romans 8:1.
12. Psalms 91:16.
13. John 15:8.
14. Matthew 5:13–14.
15. Romans 6:1–6.
16. John 16:33; Colossians 2:10.
17. Blaise Pascal, *Pensees*, trans. A. J. Krailsheimer, rev. ed. (1966; repr., London: Penguin Books, 1995), 50.
18. Eliza E. Hewitt, "When We All Get to Heaven" in William Kirkpatrick and Henry Gilmour, *Pentecostal Praises* (Philadelphia: Hall-Mack Co., 1898).
19. Psalms 100:3.

20. James 4:13–15 MSG.

21. Proverbs 3:5–6 MSG.

22. See Proverbs 13:24.

23. Matthew 6:9.

24. Hebrews 12:10.

25. v. 11.

26. Acts 13:36.

27. Psalms 81:11–12.

28. Jeremiah 7:25.

29. Carl Sagan, *Cosmos* (New York: Random House, 1980), 4.

30. Ernest Nagel, "Naturalism Reconsidered," 490.

31. Stephen Crane, *War Is Kind and Other Lines*, 1899.

10 The Real "Secret"

1. Acts 17:16.

2. Acts 17:22.

3. Acts 17:23 MSG

4. Acts 17:26.

5. Acts 17:27.

6. Acts 17:28.

7. See 2 Corinthians 5:17.

8. Ecclesiates 3:11.

9. Psalms 63:1 NLT.

10. Henry David Thoreau.

11. John 4:10.

12. John 4:13-14.

13. Romans 3:10 NLT.

14. Romans 3:23 NLT.

15. C.S. Lewis.

16. Romans 5:8 NLT.

17. Romans 3:19, *The New Testament: A New Translation* (Olaf Norlie).

18. See Galatians 3:24.

19. 2 Corinthians 4:3–4 NLT, emphasis added.

20. Colossians 1:26–28 NLT, emphasis added.

21. Isaiah 9:6.

22. 1 Corinthians 15:57.

23. See Colossians 2:10 KJV.

24. 1 John 5:12.

25. Jeremiah 2:13 NLV.

26. Nancy Arndt, unpublished, Marshfield, WI, 1983.

27. Romans 10:9.

28. John 16:13.

29. John 16:13, ICB.

30. Luke 15:7.

About the Author

Ed Gungor has been deeply involved in the spiritual formation of others for over thirty-five years. Ed is known for his down-to-earth, engaging communication style and is the author of several books, including: *Religiously Transmitted Diseases: Finding A Cure When Faith Doesn't Feel Right.* He is currently working on his fifth book, *The Vow: An Ancient Path Of Spiritual Formation That Still Transforms Today,* which is scheduled for release in early 2008 (Thomas Nelson Publishers).

Ed and his wife, Gail, of thirty years, have four children and live in Tulsa, Oklahoma. Ed currently serves as Lead Pastor at Peoples Church in Tulsa and travels around the U.S. and abroad speaking in churches, universities, and seminars.

For more information about Ed Gungor, or for additional resources by him, or to book him for speaking engagements, please visit:

www.edgungor.com

...live in response to God and his nature of love.